INSIDE
MY SHADOW BOX

INSIDE
MY SHADOW BOX

Kerrie Bullard

Library of Congress Control Number: 2014917858
ISBN: Hardcover   978-1-4990-8012-4
                 Softcover   978-1-4990-8013-1
                 eBook   978-1-4990-8014-8

Rev. date: 10/15/2014

To order additional copies of this book, contact:
Xlibris LLC
1-888-795-4274
www.Xlibris.com
Orders@Xlibris.com
663968

This book is dedicated to my parents, Joe and Jennie Ballenger. They were the first ones that held me, loved me, and nurtured me. They taught me right from wrong and instilled the values of life that I have today. Although my father is no longer here with us, his memory lives on; and the many things I loved about him continues to be a part of my daily life.

In loving memory of my grandparents, Joe and Maudie Ballenger and Will and Minnie Smith, who have given me so many fond memories as a child and an Adult. They loved me and showed me the true meaning of what a grandparent should be.

In memory of the Malones for being a very precious part of my life and for the lessons I learned from them.

To my husband, Jerry Bullard, who has always loved and supported me no matter what. He has always been there for me from the beginning in everything that I have done.

In memory of my late husband, Charlie Blair, who was one of a kind and will be always missed. There will always be a place in my heart where he lives. I'll see him again someday, but until then, I will never forget him, his laugh, and the way he was or who he was.

In memory of the late Sheriff Mickey Counts who gave me an opportunity and a beginning.

To my children and grandchildren, for the smiles and laughter that you have given me through the years. Thank you.

But most of all, I dedicate this book to God because he is always good regardless of the situation. He is always there with his perfect timing and love. He is always enough in every situation. I have not always been in the places that He wanted me to be, but He waited for me to come back to Him patiently, and welcomed me with open arms.

May God always bless and keep you. And as you read this book, I hope that it brings you some insight on how each individual part of life can hold something in it no matter how big or how small it may seem at the time.

Chapter 1

I was born on December 17, 1957, at the Simmons Memorial Hospital in Sweetwater, Texas, to a middle-class family. My dad worked, and my mom stayed home taking care of my sister and me. I was the youngest child, having one sister. I always wanted a brother but never got one. I lived a pretty normal childhood, playing mostly tomboyish games like baseball, touch football, and anything I could get by with that would allow me to hang out with my best buds of the neighborhood. Like any other child, I had hopes and dreams of what I wanted to be when I grew up. I wanted to be a nurse, a teacher, a cop, a missionary, a musician. I had a bucket list of things I wanted to be.

By the time I started first grade, my mom had started working outside of the home. I think that's the first time I felt real heartbreak—starting school and being away from Mom because she was now working. For kids today, that's the norm. But for kids in those days, having your mom work outside of the home wasn't an everyday normalcy.

My mom came to the school during a parent's visitation week and listened to me read. I remember proudly reading the sentences about Dick, Jane, Tom, Sally, and Spot. And as I finished the sentences of the part the teacher had told me to read, my mom motioned that she had to leave. She kissed and hugged me and told me how proud she was of me. It broke my heart to see my mom walk out of that classroom. I wanted to go with her. I loved my mom so much, and I always wanted to be with her. I didn't want her to leave, but I guess she had to go to work. That is the first real heartbreak that I remember. I remember wiping a tear from my eye and turning my head so that no one else would see. After all, I hadn't seen anyone else cry when their mom left.

As time went on and I got older, my dad and I became very close. We spent time together on Sunday afternoon as we rode down FM 419 to Grandma and Grandpa Ballenger's house in Fisher County, which eventually became my second home. We would talk about things we had never talked about before. My dad shared with me his wishes and dreams for me when I grew up. Dad was usually very quiet, but on those trips he would talk so much that the thirty-minute trip would pass by before I knew it. Grandma and Grandpa Ballenger had a small farm in Fisher County that they had lived on most of their married life. I loved to go there with Dad.

Grandma always kept things in her freezer, like ice cream, and things in her fridge, like sodas. Those were the things my sister and I didn't get very often at home unless it was a treat. I knew that when I went to see them, I would leave with a soda and an ice cream cone. I can still hear my grandma asking my dad, "Can she have a c-r-e-a-m cone?" I don't' think that she had caught on yet that I could spell and knew what she was asking Dad! I played along and just smiled as she asked because I knew the outcome: Daddy would say yes.

Grandma always had the coldest tea. She would make it and put it in a Marcrest tea pitcher. The pitcher was a brownstone, and I always loved the way her tea tasted and smelled in that old pitcher. She would take it straight from the fridge and pour it in the glass from the cupboard. It didn't need any ice; it was ice-cold.

At the time, I didn't realize what a treasure that old pitcher was until later in life when I was walking through an antique store and found one just like it. I found out that the stoneware was made during the Depression era and was handed out at service stations when people would buy gas.

The store clerk showed me a star and "USA" on the bottom. He said that symbolized the authenticity of it being true Marcrest. He told me the ones that had "USA" stamped on them were the oldest and that the star came later. I bought that one, and the next thing I knew, I was collecting them. I now have the full set—dishes, creamers, carafes, sugar bowls, cookie jar, and anything else I can find. Just another reminder of the treasures from Grandma's house, something I can use as a visual share with my children and grandchildren of my fond memories of Grandma and Grandpa's house.

The old farm where Grandma and Grandpa lived had a house behind it that Grandma often told me was the house that she and Grandpa lived in when my dad was born. She told me he wasn't born in a hospital, that he was born at home in that house. I couldn't fathom that. I tried to imagine how a baby would be born at home, but I was too young to understand the birthing process anyway. So I guess with time, I just learned to accept it.

Grandma's house was always full of treasures. She had lots of hats. There must have been at least fifty hats. She kept them on what my sister and I called the "hat table." She also had a dressing table with rouge, lipstick, and hair spray. My sister and I always had fun playing at Grandma's house.

Grandpa always had a quarter for my sister and me every time he would see us. I thought his pocket was an endless tunnel of quarters! Grandpa always had a red bandana to wipe his sweat as he came in from the field. I can remember thinking in the seventies when the scarf bandanas came out; Grandpa could have invented these! Even after I grew up, Grandpa would always give my children quarters, and Grandma would ask me if it was okay for them to have a c-r-e-a-m cone.

In the summer time, Grandpa would sometimes let us drive the tractor with him, and he would make swings for us from rope and tractor seats. We would help Grandma gather eggs from the hen house, but the one thing I remember most was that on the first morning that I would stay at their house, I would awaken to the smell of Grandma baking a fruit cocktail cake. She knew how much I loved them, and she made the best, and always just for me.

Grandma and Grandpa didn't have indoor plumbing at their house. I thought this was pretty cool. They had an outhouse and a cistern. The cistern was used to bring water into the house. I was never allowed to go inside the outhouse. Mom told me there might be snakes in there, so I had to go into the bushes. To me that was pretty cool because it was something different from my normal time at our house in town! When we bathed at Grandma's house, we used washbasins, and Grandma would heat the water on the stove to make sure it was warm enough.

One summer, when my sister and I went to the farm to stay with Grandma and Grandpa, it had rained. And it was still raining off and on the day we got there. When my sister and I went to the hen house with Grandma, there were these gigantic black spiders all over the place. My sister and I had never seen anything like this.

Me, being the tomboy that I was, thought, *Oh cool*. And my sister, being the girlie girl that she was, screamed, cried, and hid behind Grandma. Grandma always carried a stick with her, so she just smashed the spiders with the stick. We later found out those big spiders were tarantulas. My sister slept with her shoes on for the rest of that week because she was afraid the spiders would come in the house and get in bed with us.

Once, on a Sunday afternoon when Dad and I went to visit, Grandpa's dog was after something in the shed. When I went out to check it out, I found the dog and a skunk in there. I got there just in time to get sprayed along with the dog. Grandma tried to help by spraying lilac air freshener on me to mask the smell, but I think it made it worse.

It must have been a really long trip home with Dad because of the smell, but he never said anything or made a big deal out of it. Mom, on the other hand, made me throw my clothes away. And I don't remember how long it took me to get the smell off. I guess it's just something you get used to after a while—or not!

When I was a kid, for as long as I can remember, I loved pianos. I always admired anyone who could play one and longed to play, but Mom didn't think I would be able to stay still long enough to practice, so I never got lessons. I would watch the ladies at church as they played. I was fascinated. I longed for music. I longed to play the piano. I wanted to sing. I wanted to write songs. In the deepest of my heart, music was a love like I had never known before. I wanted to play so badly that sometimes at night I would dream that I was sitting at a piano, playing. I could feel the way the piano keys felt in my fingers, and I could almost see the hammers as they hit the strings. I could distinctly hear every note being played.

When I was in the fourth grade, Mom and Dad bought me a little chord organ for Christmas. I remember that they gave it to me early because I had been very sick with the flu, and they thought it would make me feel better. It wasn't very big, but I was in love with it. That is when I proved to Mom and Dad that I could play. I just sat down and started picking songs out. I could hear and feel the notes as I played.

Before long, I was using the chords and making music. It was an instant love for me that I knew very well and had longed for most of my life.

When Grandpa Ballenger would come to the house to visit, he would ask me to play The Old Rugged Cross. I remember working on that song so hard. I wanted to play it perfectly for Grandpa. Grandpa once told me not to ever give up. He said if you really want something, work on it until you have it. Don't ever give up. Just keep trying until you get it right. Don't settle for less because if you do, you'll never be your best. I didn't give up, and I played. After that, I proudly took requests. Dad wanted The Unclouded Day, Mom would want to hear Sweet Hour of Prayer, and of course I had to play my favorite—Jesus Loves Me. Funny thing, the same year that I got that organ, my mother's brother from California also bought me a larger chord organ with bass chords on it. I was filled with music!

Grandma and Grandpa lived in that old farm until the mid-seventies when Grandpa retired from farming and they bought a house in town. We celebrated their fiftieth anniversary in the house in town, and the old farmhouse just stayed there empty until it could no longer stand anymore, but it served its purpose. It housed a family and held many good memories.

I really never got used to the fact that they no longer lived on the farm where I had so many good memories, but I was glad for them to be closer to town as it gave Grandma a chance to do many of the things she loved doing, like socializing. She also got her long-wished-for indoor plumbing. Grandpa was happy just taking care of things around the house and visiting with the lifelong friends he had spent so many years farming with.

By now my sister had moved to Vermont. She was married and had children, and I was married and had two children. I pretty much took care of Grandma and Grandpa. I took them to the doctor when they needed to go, and I went to visit them often. I would always try to cook something special for them and take it to them when I would go to their house.

The year that I turned twenty-three, I felt one of the biggest heartaches that I had ever felt in my life. I received a phone call from my grandmother asking me if I could come that day. She said that Grandpa was having a hard time swallowing. That alerted me that something was wrong. When I got there, Grandpa was in his bed, which was very unusual. He was very dehydrated, and I called for an ambulance. I then called my dad and told him that something was very wrong with Grandpa. The doctor told us that his kidneys had started to shut down and he didn't know if anything would help at this point.

I talked to Grandpa and asked him if I could spend the night there with him. I told him that it had been a very long time since I had stayed overnight with him. I think he knew, but he didn't say it. He just took my hand and said he would like it if I stayed.

Dad was there and asked if he could stay, too, but my dad's brother decided he would stay instead. The hospital told us we could sleep in the family room, but I wanted to stay near Grandpa. I sat beside his bed through the night, holding his hand and talking to him. By now, he had lapsed into unconsciousness, but I have always heard that hearing is the last thing to leave a person when they are dying. I quietly whispered to Grandpa throughout the night that I loved him very dearly and I was there with him. I patted his hand to let him feel me there.

My uncle stayed in the family room that night. Early the next morning, my uncle came around and asked if I wanted to go for breakfast. I told him to go ahead, that I would stay there. Just after he left, my dad came. As my dad stood at the end of Grandpa's bed, we talked quietly while I held Grandpa's hand. Again, I whispered to him that I loved him and told him that Daddy was there with me. My grandfather got very quiet. His breathing changed to a very shallow pace, and then he was gone.

People say that sometimes when a person is dying, they have a wish to have certain one's that are close to be with them, and I will always believe that Grandpa waited for Daddy to get there before he left us.

My dad was his firstborn and was the one who regularly went on Sundays to see him. He was the one who helped on Grandpa's farm as he grew up.

The saddest thing was to be the one to tell Grandma that Grandpa had passed away. That is the first of two instances I remember seeing Grandmother Ballenger cry. The other time was when I had to break the news to her that my uncle had been found dead. My grandma passed away several years later. I know that her heart was broken as many times she would ask me "why"?

The night she passed away, I working on patrol in Fisher County. I received a call that she had been taken to the hospital. I spoke to my grandma on the phone and told her that I would come after my shift was over at midnight. The last thing I told her was how much I loved her. At about 11:30 p.m., I was patrolling an area in the county that had been burglarized several times in the past weeks when I noticed some headlights off in the distance. I took the dirt road leading toward the headlights and began to follow them. It seemed that I could never catch up with the headlights, and then they just vanished.

I stopped and began to look around me. I noticed I was sitting in front of the gates of my grandparent's farm. Just as I realized where I was, I received a call on my police radio telling me that I needed to go to my house for an urgent phone call. I knew, but I didn't want to believe that Grandma had passed away. I went immediately to my house and received the call from my uncle telling me that Grandma had passed away peacefully in her sleep.

Maybe that was Grandma's way of telling me goodbye. I believe she tried to wait to tell me goodbye, but it was already her time, her time to meet my grandpa in the light of their life, the place where they had raised their children and allowed their grandchildren to have so many happy times—at the old farmhouse in Fisher County. She was home. Once again they joined together and will live an eternal happy life where I will one day see them again.

Another dream that I had aside of being a musician was becoming a cop. In the mid-eighties, I was accepted into the police academy. This was an accomplishment because at this time, women were just in the beginning stages of being accepted into the academy in this area. A week after I graduated, I went to work at Nolan County Sheriff Department as a night booking officer and warrants deputy. After working there for about a year, I met Sheriff Mickey Counts from Fisher County. He told me that if I ever decided to leave Nolan County, he would be interested in hiring me in Fisher County. Shortly after meeting Sheriff Counts, I quit working for Nolan County. Something just didn't seem right in Nolan County, and I later found out that the sheriff was doing some things that were illegal. He was eventually arrested and served federal time for his deeds.

Fisher County has always been my home away from home because of the many visits I made to my grandparent's house, so after I quit working at Nolan County Sheriff Department, I contacted Sheriff Counts. He told me that he had an opening, and I took the position.

Much to my surprise, I found out that I was going to be the first female commissioned patrol officer for Fisher County. To me, that was a great honor—just to be a part of that history, the first female deputy sheriff in Fisher County. That job lasted through most of my career as a deputy. Not only did I work for Sheriff Counts but also for Sheriff Gene Pack as well in Fisher County.

I loved living in and raising my children in Fisher County. I often took my children to the gates of the farm where I spent so many summers and enjoyed my Grandma's fruit cocktail cake, to a place where there were cool summer breezes blowing into the windows as I slept beside my grandma at night and smelled the fresh plowed ground of Fisher County. I spoke often of the wonders that this place held for me as a child so that they would know and remember my heritage.

Although both of my children had the opportunity to know my grandparents before they died, they did not get to know them in the sweet sense that I had known them as a child. They did not have the opportunity to drink the tea from the Marcrest pitcher, swing on a swing made by my grandfather, smell the cool summer breezes as they blew through the windows of Grandma's house, or know the sweet taste of Grandma's fruit cocktail cakes. My children have often told me how proud they were to have grown up in the small town setting in Fisher County and to have gotten to know the roots of their family.

Grandma Smith lived in the little town in Merkel, Texas. I don't remember much about my grandfather in Merkel because he died when I was about four years old. I do remember that he was tall, that he walked very slowly when he walked through a door, and that he smoked a pipe. I always spent some of the summer at her house too. I'm not sure how she did it because she didn't have much money, but she always managed to make the best meals for my sister, my cousins, and me. I think Grandma Smith made the best buttermilk biscuits that I have ever eaten, and she always had the coldest buttermilk in her fridge. I wasn't really a fan of buttermilk, but at her house, I always made it a point to drink a glass.

Merkel is a small town with friendly people who always smile and speak, even to a stranger. Being there gave me a feeling of being at home, and I always looked forward to visiting there. Going shopping with Grandma Smith to Carson's Supermarket was always a treat. I can still remember the smell of freshly barbequing chicken in the deli, and

I can still imagine the cold air from the air-conditioner in the store. I remember going barefoot as we walked through the brick streets of the downtown district. Today the streets are still brick, and most of the buildings that were there when I was a child still stand.

Back in those days, not many had refrigerated air-conditioning; mostly swamp coolers, if there was air-conditioning at all. I remember at Grandma's house, there was no air-conditioner. She propped open her windows with a peg-like stick, and we had to be careful not to knock the stick out if we were near the window because it would end up closing on an arm, and that really hurt.

My grandmother was good at just about anything she did—gardening, sewing, cooking, and especially whistling. She always whistled hymns while she cleaned or cooked. Her favorite hymn was "What a Friend We Have in Jesus." I learned to play it for her on my organ. I can still hear her telling people as I played that I had never taken a lesson in my life and that I had just learned to play because God gave me a gift.

The house my grandma in Merkel lived in was the house that she had lived in most of her married life. It was a white frame house with a porch all the way across the front. Oh, the times we as a family had at that house, gathering on holidays and for family events. The house was filled with people talking, smells of food, and sounds of children running in and out the front screen door, slamming it each time. It may have been crowded, but we never realized it; we just enjoyed it. The house must have been built in the early 1900s or late 1800s. Grandma and Grandpa raised eleven children in that house. When they bought the house, there were only a few rooms in the house. My uncle, who was an architect, would later build on to the house, giving Grandma much more room. This was done after my grandpa passed away.

My uncle Robert, who was an architect, had a terrible accident in the early sixties that left him without legs. I can still remember seeing him as he worked on Grandma's house without legs. He used his arms. It was an amazing sight of strength that I will never forget as he moved from place to place, handling his tools, using only his arms. I can't imagine what it took for him to learn that skill alone. He is one of my true heroes because he did not let his handicap overcome his will to do what he loved.

When the television series *The Waltons* came on, my mom would always say that the Walton family reminded her of her own family and that Uncle Robert was the "John Boy" of their family because in *The Waltons*, John Boy was always the one who stepped up to help when someone needed help—and Uncle Robert was just like that. I believe every family has a "John Boy" in it, or at least that's my hope.

Grandma always had the best garden in the summer. When she would water the garden, it was always a treat for me and my cousins to be outside because she would spray us with the water hose. The water was always so cold because she had a water well. I can still hear her laughing as we would screech at the feel of the cold water as we ran around waiting for her to spray us again—screeches of laughter and play of days now gone. She did special things with us, like help us to sew aprons and curtains, and she always had a homemade bonnet to wear in her garden.

When Grandpa was still alive, Grandma had hair that went to the back of her knees, but she cut it shortly after his death. She used to tell me that it would never dry before she had to wash it again and that she had promised my grandpa she wouldn't ever cut it until after he was gone. She said cutting her hair made life easier for her. I often wondered what Grandma Smith looked like in her younger days. I have never seen any pictures of her before she was my grandma.

At Christmastime at Grandma Smith's house, there was always a large crowd when I was a child. The house was filled with talking aunts and uncles, laughing cousins, smells of food cooking, dishes rattling, and Grandma's whistling. I made my first fruit salad there on a Christmas. It has been a tradition that I make the fruit salad every Christmas since!

Grandma had an old antique buffet where all of the food was placed as we lined up to fill our plates with all of the different foods that everyone brought and prepared at Grandma's house. For the most part, Uncle Bill, Aunt Minnie, and their two boys; Uncle Carl, Aunt Francis, and their five children; Aunt Lovetta, Uncle Butch, and their five children; Mom, Dad, me, and my sister; Aunt Jean, Uncle Ervin, and their three kids; Uncle Alvin, Aunt Marilyn, and their three girls; and three or four of my great aunts and uncles would be there along with Grandma and Aunt Ora Vee. In that small house, there was a lot of people, but only a portion of what it could be if the whole family showed.

Aunt Ora Vee was special. She was an adult but was like a playmate to me and my cousins. She wasn't mentally handicapped; she was just a little slow and unable to care for herself. When it came to all of us children, she had the patience of Job and loved having us around. I've heard it said that God chooses special people to care for special people. In this case, he did because no one could have ever taken care of Aunt Ora Vee like Grandma Smith did, and no one could have cared for my grandma like Aunt Ora Vee did. I once asked Grandma Smith where she came up with the name "Ora Vee," and she said she always wanted to have daughters named Ora Vee and Jennie Marie. Jennie Marie would be my mom.

When I was young, Grandma Smith didn't have a washer at her house, so we had to go to the laundromat. Since Grandma didn't drive and had no car, the owner of the laundromat, Mr. West, would pick up Grandma, Ora Vee, my sister, my three cousins, and me and take us to the laundromat. Mr. West was a really nice man. Sometimes, he would let me, my sister, or one of my cousins help him drive his car to the laundromat. When we got there, he would always open up the Coke machine and give each one of us an ice-cold coke. That in itself was a treat.

The Borden's milk truck came once a week to Grandma's house, and we knew when he came, there would be a treat in that too. The poor milk truck driver would be bombarded by my sister, me, and my three cousins when he drove up asking all kinds of questions. He was always very nice. After he left, Grandma Smith would hand out Dixie Doodle ice cream bars that she had purchased to each of us. That sure made the hot afternoons a lot cooler.

I remember one time in Sweetwater, I saw this Borden's truck driver that looked a lot like the one my grandma had. I asked him if he knew Ora Vee. He must have thought I was a crazy little kid, but he just smiled and answered that he knew lots of Ora Vee's.

When my cousins and I wanted to go to town, Aunt Ora Vee would walk with us. Everyone knew Aunt Ora Vee, and she knew everyone. One time, it was just me and Aunt Ora Vee that walked into town, and I remember when we got back to near Grandma's house, I began to see large drops of blood all over the place. It had rained that week, and there were mud puddles everywhere; and where there was a mud puddle, there were pollywogs. It seemed that my cousin had gotten one of Grandma's canning jars to catch pollywogs and broken it, cutting her foot.

When she got to Grandma's with her wounded foot, she got Grandma's traditional medicinal treatment on the wound. Grandma believed that bleeding could be stopped with sugar, and the wound could be cleaned with alcohol. Anytime anyone got hurt at Grandma Smith's, they would be treated with sugar and alcohol, followed by getting the wound wrapped in some of her special material.

I remember once on a Christmas time at Grandma Smith's house, I was playing touch football with some of my cousins when I ran through Grandma's barbed wire fence where she had her goats. I hid in the bathroom because I knew she was going to get out the sugar and alcohol. Unfortunately, my tattletale cousin told her where I was. Out of all of the injuries that I got as a child, that one healed better than most did.

Evening time at Grandma Smith's was pretty simple for us. Sometimes, my great aunts would come for a visit, and I would sit at my chord organ that Uncle Robert had given me and take requests of their favorite hymns, and everyone would sing along. In the daytime, Grandma always had her radio on for the Bill Barnet show. Grandma would ask me to call in her request of Coat of Many Colors. I loved calling in to that show because sometimes, Mr. Barnet would replay the phone conversation, and I got to hear my voice on the radio! When Mom and Dad told me that I had to give my beagle, Tiger, away, I gave him to Mr. Barnett because on one of his radio shows, Mr. Barnet mentioned that he wanted a dog. I called him, and he took Tiger. From time to time, Mr. Barnet would mention Tiger so that I would know that he was in good hands.

Aunt Ora Vee was, for the most part, always happy; but sometimes she would become angry with Grandma Smith. Grandma Smith could usually get her calmed down, but on one particular incident after I had grown up, Grandma Smith was unable to calm her. This was when Aunt Ora Vee had to be placed in a nursing home, and Grandma Smith moved from her home in Merkel, Texas, to a house near my aunt Lovetta in Crockett, Texas. After this, I didn't get to see my grandma or Aunt Ora Vee as often because of the distance between us. Aunt Ora Vee was taken to Oklahoma where my mom's brothers lived.

Things forever changed. No more trips to Carson's Supermarket, no more sugar and alcohol, no more trips to the laundromat, no more Dixie Doodles, and no more Christmases at Grandma's. After all, I had grown into an adult. But as the saying goes, "You don't know what you have until it's gone." It is very true.

I went to see Grandma several times in Crockett, Texas, and finally she had to go into a nursing home. She had begun to have some dementia. I saw Grandma not long before she passed away, and I think she recognized me. She told me and my cousin that there was no need for us to have traveled so far to see her, and both of us thought we heard her mention our name. I know this for sure, that she did whisper very sweetly in her own time, "What a friend we have in Jesus."

Aunt Ora Vee passed away in the year 2000, a few years after Grandma did. I took my mom to Oklahoma to see her about a month before she passed away, and she knew me as soon as she saw me walk into her room. I had not seen her in the years since she had left the little town of Merkel, Texas. Aunt Ora Vee was dying with cancer. She asked me if I thought she was going to die soon, and I remember telling her that even if she left this earth, the memory of her would live on forever in my mind. This brought a smile to her face, and then she asked me if I would play the piano for her. I rolled her wheelchair down to the foyer of the nursing home and asked her to give me a request. She requested that I play "For God So Loved the World."

As I played, Aunt Ora Vee sang the song in her very weak voice with a smiling face. When we got through with the song, I heard applauses from behind us, and that's when we discovered that my playing had summoned the nursing home patients and nurses to the foyer. I stayed there for the remainder of that afternoon, taking requests and playing as the residents of the nursing home sang their favorite hymns, and Aunt Ora Vee directed. It was a simple time but a very memorable one, a time that will live forever in my memory and maybe a time that made some people happy for the afternoon.

As my mom and I left from the nursing home, Aunt Ora Vee asked if she could pray before we left, so we all prayed. She asked God to watch over us and take control of the trip home to keep us safe. Little did I know that the prayer she prayed was a much-needed prayer because as Mom and I got on the highway, my vision became blurred; and by the time I got home, my eyes were on fire. I had probably handled a wheelchair or something at the nursing home that passed on conjunctivitis to my eyes. My vision was not blurred when we left the nursing home, and I will never forget Aunt Ora Vee sitting in the doorway waving goodbye to us and telling us not to be so long in coming to see her the next time. She passed away within a few weeks. I sang at her funeral, and played the piano. I think she would have wanted that.

Those times in Merkel, Texas, as a child were simple times where I got a lot of living out of life. I learned to know and appreciate that in life, you do not have to have material things to enjoy things; you just have to be a part of whatever is there for you.

The old house where Grandma lived for so many years is now gone. Some kids were playing with candles and set it on fire. I can still see the rooms of the house in my mind. Recently, when my sister had a reunion for the family at her house, I sat quietly in her living room and listened to the familiar sounds of children running through the house playing, cousins and aunts talking, dishes rattling, and the smell of food cooking. As I sat, I held my infant great nephew very close to me and thought to myself that the only thing missing from this scene is the distant whistling of "What a Friend We Have in Jesus." So I quietly whistled it to him while he took his bottle. I don't know if I did the song as much justice as Grandma did, but this I know: my nephew smiled sweetly as he drifted off to sleep.

I've heard it said that when a new baby smiles in their sleep, they are dreaming of angels—maybe those from the past who have gone on to heaven were there when my great nephew smiled gently whispering the fond memories of the past to him, especially those who started the traditions of family gatherings many years ago. Maybe my great nephew got a glimpse of what we had as children growing up in Grandma's little house in Merkel, Texas, or on that old farmhouse in Fisher County. My hope is that he will smile often in his sleep with those peaceful glances at what was then, and what will hopefully remain

Mom holding me as an infant

My father in his army uniform

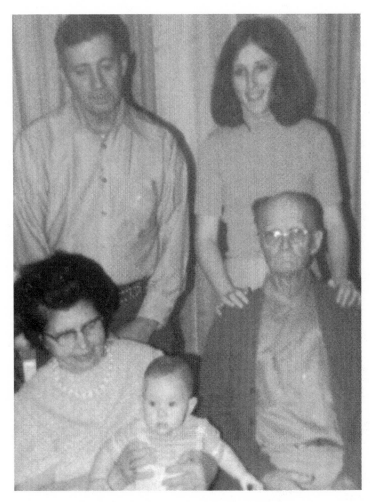

Four generations: Grandpa & Grandma
Ballenger, Dad, Me, and my son

Grandpa & Grandma Smith

Grandma Smith and Ora Vee

Decedents of the Smith family at Grandma Smith's
house in front of home in mid 70's

Smith family reunion 2014

Kerrie with Sweetwater High School Stage Band in 1973

A baby's smile

Chapter 2

Meeting the Malones was a piece of my life that really made an impact. Mr. Malone was known as the neighborhood grump according to the kids in the neighborhood, but I soon found that from the first time I met him that I would grow to love him almost as much as I did my own grandparents.

Mr. Malone had a house about a block from my house, and I could see his house across the vacant lot near my house. His wife's name was Cora, but he called her Fannie. I really never knew why he had that nickname for her, but sometimes she would kind of scowl at him when he called her that. Their home wasn't anything fancy, but it was very nice and had air-conditioning with refrigerated air. I thought that was pretty cool, especially on the hot Saturday afternoons when I would visit.

My first meeting with Mr. Malone was kind of unusual. My friend Terry and I were playing around the neighborhood when we stumbled up on a bunch of dead birds. We later found out that they were just a few of Mr. Malone's flock of animals. He was definitely one to have a love for animals as I would soon learn. Mr. Malone at first sounded very gruff as he asked Terry and me if we were responsible for killing his birds. But once he knew that we were totally innocent of the act, he became a very nice man and eventually offered me one of his Chihuahua dogs. I took him up on the offer before asking my mom, which didn't please her too much. But we made the best out of a bad situation and kept the dog, and we named him Skippy!

Mr. Malone was there through the heartbreak of losing Skippy during the Christmas break of that year. It seems that while my sister and I were out of school visiting our grandmother, Skippy decided to go to the school to look for us, and he was struck by a car. I can remember the endless hours of calling out for him, wandering up and down the streets in our neighborhood looking for him. Mr. Malone got in his car and canvassed the neighborhood looking for him also. But on our way back to school, we found him on a vacant lot near the school. He was dead. And when I got home from school, my mom said my eyes were nearly swollen shut from crying all day. Mr. Malone must have known that I was totally heartbroken because he immediately replaced Skippy with another dog named Spot. He told me that I should take care of her and love her like I had loved Skippy, and I did.

It was always a thrill to get to go and see the Malones. Mr. Malone had a very nice backyard, and then another section of his yard was fenced off. In that yard, Mr. Malone had prairie dogs, rabbits, his dogs, some chickens, and pigeons. It was almost as good as going to the zoo. Most of the animals were animals that Mr. Malone had rescued in some way or another. He told me the prairie dogs had lived on one of the vacant lots nearby until people started setting traps and destroying them, so he began taking them in and caring for them so they would not be harmed.

He told me that animals need to be loved just like people do and that although most wild animals have their own instincts to stay alive, when their natural habitat is taken from them, they become helpless. The rabbits, he told me, were injured; and he had nursed them back to health. He said he had just continued to keep them because they became dependent on him to care for them.

After Spot was gone, Mr. Malone came to my rescue again with Tubby. Tubby came to be a very big part of our family's life. He lived fourteen years. I was seven when I got him and twenty-one when he died. It was a heartbreaking moment for me when we lost him. He actually outlived Mr. Malone, so when Tubby died, it was like losing Mr. Malone all over again. This time, Mr. Malone was not there to fix the hurt or give me another puppy to help with the pain. It was a very hard loss for me. But this I know: Tubby died old, cared for, and much loved.

Mr. Malone had a garage that he had converted into his own space. He had a HAM radio in there, and sometimes he would let me talk to his radio buddies. It was exciting to get to talk on that radio. I can still remember his radio call letters even after all of these years: W5GFN. The radio numbers hung on a tag above his shed door.

Mrs. Malone was a little different, but she was always nice to me. She would usually offer me a cold drink of tea or lemon aid when I went to the house. I think my visits became a part of their life very quickly, and they became a part of my heart very quickly. I loved them both very much, although it would take me longer to get attached to Mrs. Malone.

Although I was very young and didn't quite understand what a blood clot was, Mr. Malone developed one behind his eyes. He told me about it, but I really didn't think much about it until he started losing his sight. His driving became slower as he traveled down our streets, and I remember telling him that he should drive a little faster because he was going to get run over by someone.

When I saw the ambulance at his house, I remember racing toward his house. I didn't care about anything except trying to help the Malones. I didn't know that Mr. Malone had passed away. I can remember being at his funeral and hearing the preacher saying that Mr. Malone didn't attend church very often, but he believed that Mr. Malone was in heaven because of the heart Mr. Malone had. He said that God has certain people that he chooses to do certain things, and he believed that God had chosen Mr. Malone to help take care of crippled animals.

He said that with a heart for animals like Mr. Malone had, he believed that God and Mr. Malone's natural instinct to love was in it. I remember that these kind words from the preacher made it easier for me to think that Mr. Malone was in heaven with God, Skippy, Spot, and Tubby. He said that God gives people certain tasks, and he believed that Mr. Malone had fulfilled those tasks in caring for the little creatures as he did. The preacher was right in that Mr. Malone would never allow an animal to suffer. He would always take them in and do whatever he could to nurse them back to health. If he failed, he would be very sad and talk about it with me.

The one thing I learned from Mr. Malone is to always respect an animal in the sense that you as a person would want to be respected. He once told me that animals have feelings and needs just like people do. I have never forgotten that. I believe that Mr. Malone took all of the feelings he held inside and shared them with his animals. Maybe it was in the times that he was alone with them and feeding them, or the times when he found them injured, or maybe just in the quiet of the morning. But whenever it was, it was evident that he had a special bond with them. A bond that most wouldn't understand, but I did because I felt the same way.

I have always been one who would stop on the side of the road and help an injured animal if I could or try to find a home for an orphaned cat or dog. I have taken in baby birds that have fallen from their nests and fed them until they were strong enough to fly away on their own.

From Mr. Malone, I learned that sometimes God just gives you the little animals to love and nurture. And when he does, I know it's his way of saying to me, "Here it is, take care of it for me. Let others see me through your caring attitude." Like what the preacher said at Mr. Malone's funeral, God's hand picks people to take these tasks and do them. I'm glad he picks me sometimes. There's a song that I sing entitled "His Eye is on the Sparrow," and I know he watches me and all living things.

Mrs. Malone and I kept in contact after Mr. Malone passed away. I continued my Saturday visits with her regularly. Mrs. Malone told me that she had turned all of the animals loose. It was kind of hard to go to their house and not see all of the little animals that I had learned to love so much through the years. I was fourteen the summer after Mr. Malone passed away. That summer, Mrs. Malone called my mom to see if she would let me go with her to Knox City, Texas, to visit with her sister there. Mrs. Malone explained to my mom that she didn't want to make the trip alone, and my mom agreed to let me go.

When we got to her sister's house, it seemed like we were in the middle of nowhere. I wasn't sure if I would like this place or not, but I soon found myself at home in the den of their home. They had a piano! I loved pianos!

Mr. and Mrs. Parkhill were special. I grew to love them both very quickly during that time I was at their house. I soon found that Mr. Parkhill could play the piano; so he would play, and I would sing. I think they all must have had a lot of patience, being around a fourteen-year-old in the middle of nowhere, just trying to keep me occupied! I know I must have bugged them all at one time or another for some reason or another! Every day, Mr. Parkhill would turn on the irrigation system to their farm. I loved it because it was paved ditch and had the coldest water.

Mr. Parkhill would tell me before he turned on the water, and I would get my bathing suit on and sit in the irrigation ditch and let the cold water flow over me. It reminded me of the times that Grandma Smith would spray me with her well water. It was fun, it was cold, and it was a time that I will never forget! Every day we would have fresh cantaloupes and fresh vegetables from their garden. They were the best that I had ever eaten. I loved meal time at their house. It was unforgettable, and it seemed like I could never get enough of that sweet cantaloupe.

Little did I know that the best was yet to come: Mrs. Parkhill would make fresh homemade peach ice cream that has since stayed in my memory. She used fresh cream from their farm and peaches from their orchard. It was the best. I have never eaten ice cream so good. How I wish I could go back in time and eat ice cream with them again. After we ate ice cream, we would all put on our bathing suits and go to the cement tank and sit and talk. It was a good time. I learned about times when they were young and about their loves and disappointments in life. We talked about Mr. Malone and all of the things we loved about him.

You wouldn't think a fourteen-year-old girl would enjoy being around older people talking about past times, but I loved every minute of it. I was never bored with them. They were interesting and funny. We talked about Mr. Malone and how much we missed him. It was as much therapy for me as it was for Mrs. Malone. It was a time for healing for us both as well as a time for bonding for us both. Although I had visited with Mr. and Mrs. Malone on many occasions, I had really spent the majority of the time with Mr. Malone. After the summer visit to the Parkhills, I became very attached to Mrs. Malone and visited her as often as I could, mostly every week.

The year I turned sixteen, my neighbor called me and asked if I had seen the ambulance she had seen at Mrs. Malone's house. It was like reliving the nightmare of when Mr. Malone had passed away. I raced down to her house as they were loading her into the ambulance, and I was met by another friend. It seems that Mrs. Malone had fallen in her bathtub. She had lain there for a couple of days before anyone found her because she had broken her hip.

I was so sad. I had been by her house on Sunday afternoon, but she didn't answer her door. I wondered if she had been in that bathtub needing my help when I went by. Why didn't I just open the door and call to her? I blamed myself for the longest time for her suffering. My heart was saddened as I went to the hospital to see her. I brushed her hair and talked to her. I don't think she really knew me, but at least I could be near her. Later they moved her to the nursing home. I visited with her, and the nurses told me she wouldn't eat for them. I was able to get her to eat everything on her plate. I had new hope that she would be okay, but she wasn't. She died the next week.

After her funeral, I went to her house. Her daughter from California was there taking care of getting all of her stuff out of the house. I can still see what her house looked like when she was there and what it looked like when she wasn't there. My heart ached, and her daughter must have sensed it. She gave me a few of Mrs. Malone's personal things, like some fans she had hanging on her wall and a bible that Mrs. Malone had written in. I loved Mr. and Mrs. Malone as if they were my family. I speak of them often and call them my other grandparents because that's what they were to me. I believe they both loved me as much as I loved them.

From Mrs. Malone, I learned that although one may seem harsh at first, you shouldn't judge that book by its cover because somewhere in the midst of the book you will find changes. Mrs. Malone was as soft and sweet as the ice cream we had eaten at her sister's house, but yet as harsh as the cold water hitting me on the legs as it came rushing down the irrigation ditch that summer. And although she was harsh at times, the softness of her heart came through in the end.

I went back to see the Parkhills one more time after I grew up and got married. Their farm had not changed nor had the interiors of the rooms in the house. The kitchen was the same. The table where we had shared so many good meals was in the same place, and I could envision us as we sat at the table eating cantaloupe and peach ice cream. I smiled as I looked at the empty chairs that we all once sat in. It was a bittersweet moment because I knew that those times were gone and there would never be that kind of laughter and happiness in that sense again.

We sat in the den where the old piano still sat in the same place as it had when I was fourteen years old. I asked Mr. Parkhill to play "His Eye is on the Sparrow" for me, and I sang it softly as he played, thinking of a time when I met two of the most extraordinary people that God had allowed me to have in my life. I realized at that moment just how lucky I had been, just knowing them and loving them as I had—one of God's true gifts that I am truly grateful for.

The Parkhills let me walk through the house that day. As I walked into the room that Mrs. Malone and I had once shared, I could hear the ringing of our laughter while we talked into the night as we fell asleep. It gave my heart some peace and made me feel somehow once again like she was there. I stood in the room for a few minutes and took it all in so that I would never forget what that summer visit meant to me. For that is where Mrs. Malone and I had spent some very peaceful and healing hours during our visit. I left their house that day with the feeling that Mr. and Mrs. Malone would always be with me, even if they are millions of miles away in heaven. I know without a doubt that they will know me and recognize me when I get there.

Mr. Malone has probably been taking care of all of my pets that have gone on before me; and Mrs. Malone, well, she is probably just impatiently waiting for me so that we can laugh and catch up on everything. I know the Parkhills will be there too.

Not long ago, I was talking with a man from Knox City, Texas, whose farm is directly across the road from the Parkhills' old farm. He told me that the Parkhills had been long gone, but their house was still standing. He remembered them well and spoke of their wonderful fresh peaches and cantaloupes of past. Maybe I will go back there again and walk down memory lane once again someday. It probably isn't the same, and I am sure that all of the old furniture is gone, but it's still a memory. Maybe I will take my grandchildren with me so that they can get a glimpse of the rareness that I had in that summertime visit.

The Malones' house still stands in the old neighborhood with no one living in it. I get sad when I look in that direction knowing how it was then and see how it is now. Seeing it the way it is now makes me sad, but in the same sense, I have never forgotten how wonderful it was then.

Time does not stand still in any sense. I believe that you should live every moment in the moment and forever cherish the memories of the good times of your life, that you should share them often with those you love so that they are never forgotten and will be passed down for generations to come and so that you can feel those very precious times often.

Chapter 3

Growing up in the small town of Sweetwater, Texas, was one of the easiest tasks that I could have ever done in life. The familiar surroundings of the neighborhood consisted of homes of friends that I had visited many times, streets that I had traveled thousands of times, and faces of people that I had known all of my life. Everyone my age looked forward to the evenings on the drag downtown. Those were the free and easy days of being a teenager and having no cares except for taking the next day's exam at school or deciding what to wear to school.

It was a night of driving down East Broadway: around the courthouse, back down Broadway, around Ray's Drive In, and then to the village parking lot to meet up with your friends. The sweet days of the seventies. The sweet days of being a teenage wild child with no cares in the world.

The village parking lot derived its name from the local supermarket that was housed on that parking lot basically in the center of town—the largest supermarket in town with a big red "V" sign on the parking lot. The sign towered above the city and could be seen driving in from any direction, especially at night when the sign was lighted up in red.

Today many may wonder why the current store, Brookshire's, houses that sign on its parking lot. The sign itself is the original village sign and was moved to its current spot when the village grew and moved to the location that now houses Brookshire's supermarket. I guess Brookshire's decided not to mess with history! I would say the "V" is a landmark for Sweetwater. It has been a part of the town for as long as I can remember!

It was on the parking lot of the village where many of us met our "true loves." Most of us were sixteen and just beginning to drive, not to mention that we really had no experience at life, although we thought we were well-experienced at our age. After all, we had our driver's licenses. That made us all grown up, right?

In those days, it was called "going steady," unlike the many terms used today. The village parking lot is where I met Jeffery. Jeffery gave me his senior ring on about our third date on the village parking lot. He was such a handsome man, nineteen, out of school, and driving a beautiful 1973 Nova Super Sport. It was hunter green with black interior. Things just seemed to be perfect. He was cool, I was in love with him, and it was the best of times. Or was it?

Jeffery and I dated about a year when he informed me that he was going to visit friends in Dallas and that he was going on a blind date while there. He told me not to fret because it didn't mean anything, just something that his friend had lined up for him. He told me not to worry about it, to just stay home and wait because he would be back.

Wait, not on your life! This peaceful easy feeling that I had felt for Jeffery turned to a hateful angry feeling. Just the thought of him with someone else hurt me with a sting, harsher than anything I could ever imagine. That weekend, I drowned my pain by going to a teen dance at the Colonial Hatchery with my friends. The Colonial Hatchery was a teen hangout that had been created by the local Jaycees, and once a month they brought in a band to play a teen dance.

Admission was only a dollar. If the band was a good one, we would all stay; and if it was not so good, back to the drag and hang out with those who were there on the village parking lot. That night, we left and went back to the drag and to the parking lot on the village. That's where I met Tim.

Tim had a way of just attracting people to him. He spoke with such a suave manner when he spoke to me. He was certainly brilliant at getting my attention! Tim was twenty-one and had a brand new blue 1974 Malibu Classic. It had cruise control and an eight-track player. We made the drag a few times and decided to go back to the dance. I didn't feel like I was betraying Jeffery because he had already betrayed me with what he had done. Tim made me feel better than I had felt in a long time. He was sweet, he was cute, and he was everything I wanted Jeffery to be. But I knew in my heart that Jeffery wasn't anything like Tim.

I had already made up my mind that I was going to break it off with Jeffery because he was not true to me. Who knows how many times he would not be true to me if he was doing things this way now? It was so nonchalant to him. He could have backed out of the thing in Dallas if he really cared about us, so it was over as far as I was concerned.

I made the best of the evening and began to get to know Tim. He was such a nice gentleman to me. He just listened as I talked, and we laughed a lot. He didn't try to get intimate with me; we were more like old buddies just having a nice time in Sweetwater, Texas. It was as if I knew him and he knew me although we had just met. Tim dropped me off at my house later that night after the dance, and we just said good-bye to each other. There was nothing really special about our good-bye, except when Tim told me that he would like to see me again. I didn't give him an answer right away but told him that I would see him on the drag again sometime.

I didn't see or talk to Jeffery again until Monday morning. I knew I had to make a quick clean breakup with him, and I did. I explained to him that I felt he had betrayed our trust in each other by going out with someone else, even if it had been arranged by his friends. I told him that he could have told them no but chose to go out with someone else. It didn't even hurt me. Jeffery, on the other hand, could not believe I was ending it with him. He told me he planned on getting engaged by the end of the summer and marrying me when I got out of high school. All I could say to him was that if he was that serious about us, he should have considered it before making plans with his friends to go out with another girl. I told him going steady with a person has meaning to it—steady, not off and on when it's convenient.

Just as quickly as we met, we parted, and it was over. It hurt some, but not as badly as it had hurt me when he told me he was going to see another girl in Dallas and it didn't mean anything. It did to me. It meant everything we had. I think the initial hurt had really passed, and although the sting was still there, healing had already begun on my part. I didn't see Jeffery after that for a long time.

That night on the drag, on the village parking lot, I ran into Tim. We made a few drags listening to my favorite—Conway Twitty and Loretta Lynn. I could not believe he listened to the same music that I loved. We both laughed and sang along with the tapes. We were as comfortable together as a pair of comfortable shoes. We just fit well, it seemed. For me, this would be the last of the loves that I met on the village parking lot.

I married Tim in December 1974. I was barely seventeen. It was the very best of times for me. Tim had a great job, we liked all of the same things, we were happy, and by now we were expecting our first child. My son was born on May 28, 1975, by cesarean section after five days of struggling to get him here. The doctor had told us the night before he was born that if I didn't have the section, my baby would rupture my uterine sac and both of us would die.

There are two things I remember after they woke me up from the section: I didn't hear a baby crying, and the pain was excruciating. My first question was, "Is my baby alive?" The nurses reassured me that he was fine and they had taken him to the incubator to warm him. I could have breathed a sigh of relief, except that it hurt so badly. They brought my son to me shortly afterward and let me kiss him. I remember that my lips were so dry from not having anything to drink in so long that when I kissed him, he was wet, and it wet my lips. That is the sweetest memory I will ever have in my life: the fresh, clean, cool feeling of my lips pressing against my brand-new son.

I remember that Tim and I cried tears of relief—relief that all of the laboring was over and relief that our son was born healthy and alive. My son was beautiful. He had a headful of black hair, beautiful blue eyes, and the most beautiful round head. He seemed perfect. Just seeing him took all of the pain away, and I didn't hurt anymore.

It hadn't hit me yet that although I had given birth to this beautiful baby; I was a mother at seventeen. What did that mean? I had no idea that it would mean endless nights of colic, endless nights of worry, and no more freedom to just be me at seventeen. I know that wanting to be me at seventeen is a selfish statement, but I was still a baby myself when I had a child. Having a child at seventeen was not something I had planned. It was just something that happened.

My mom and dad told me that it was now my responsibility to care for this baby and love him as they had cared for and loved me. I had no problem with loving this baby and no problem with caring for this baby. I just had to learn how to be the mom that I needed to be to him. For the first six months of his life, he had colic. He would cry all night long every night. It seemed like an eternity with the colic. Sometimes my mom would help, but she worked and couldn't always be there. Tim worked nights and wasn't there either. I had it all to myself.

Finally, at six months old, he began to sleep most of the night. It was such a relief not only because of being sleep-deprived but because it meant that my baby wasn't hurting anymore. He was a happy baby for the most part after he got over the colic episodes, but he did not like to entertain himself. He wanted my full attention. He didn't like playing with his toys; he wanted me in the floor playing with him. I was a full-time mother and wife.

By now, we had joined a church, and it was a very big part of our lives. We looked forward to attending each week. My son loved going to the nursery. I was able to use my voice for God. Our Sunday school class was wonderful, and life was at its best. A lady in the church became my friend. She was close to my age, and her husband became friends with Tim. They had three boys, and we all became very close. We had dinner together, went to movies together, and always sat together in church. Her husband travelled with his job a lot, and she was left at home to care for the three boys alone. I felt for her because it seemed that she had little time for herself, so she and I began trading out babysitting time. I would keep her boys while she went out for an afternoon, and she would keep my son when I went out. It worked out pretty well.

By now, Tim and I had bought a house and were talking about having another baby. My son was past potty training, had broken from his bottle, and was talking well. Life seemed pretty good until one day when everything changed the course of our future.

I remember that my "friend" was supposed to take my son that afternoon but called to tell me that her husband had gone out of town unexpectedly. She said the boys had gone over to a friend's house and she wasn't feeling up to keeping my son that day. About three or four weeks prior to this, my "friend" had started making some derogatory remarks about Tim and how he really needed to learn to treat me better. I didn't know what she was talking about, but I was going to find out soon enough.

Tim had gotten home early because he was working the day shift that day. I asked him to watch our son so I could go to the store, but he told me that he was going to see my "friend's" husband, that they had made some plans. It kind of went over my head until after he left. I thought to myself about my earlier conversation with her about her husband leaving town unexpectedly. I took my son to my mom's house and drove over to her house. It was no surprise to me when I found

Tim's pickup parked in her drive. I rang the doorbell, and she came to the door in her robe.

I asked her where Tim was, and he was standing behind her, but he was fully dressed. I just turned around and walked away. I was angry, hurt, disappointed, confused; so many feelings were surfacing that I don't even know how far I had gotten down her sidewalk when I realized that Tim was right behind me. I remember her saying something, but I don't remember what she said. Tim was asking me to stop as I headed for my car. He was pleading with me. I told him that I just couldn't handle this right now and to stay away from me, and I left.

I didn't know what to do except get my son and head home. When I got to my mom's house, I don't know if she could tell by the hurt look on my face or if she had suspected what was going on, but she knew. She was very understanding and tried to comfort me as we talked about this. She said that she had noticed some things at church that led her to believe that something was going on with Tim and my "friend".

I went home and talked to Tim about my feelings. He seemed sincere that this had been going on for just a short time, but I wasn't so sure. My trust had gone down to a very low level. I tried very hard to forgive Tim for this but my trust level had just dissipated. I stayed at our house and Tim moved to the guest bedroom.

It was almost as if everything that Tim and I had shared had been flushed swiftly down the toilet. I filed for divorce, and Tim moved out into his parents' house.

By now, I had gotten my certification for an Emergency Medical Technician, so I was working part time for the local ambulance. My mom would help me with my son when I had to make night transports, and she would keep him at her house.

There were many nights that I heard people walking around my bedroom window in the night, sometimes knocking on my window. I felt that I had to move away to get away from all of this. I got a job at Midland Memorial Hospital and moved in with my aunt who lived there. Tim had visitation rights with our son, so I would have my mom take him, and then I would go and pick him up on my days off. It was a very dark and sad time in my life and a very confusing time in my son's life.

Shortly after I moved to Midland, I found out I was pregnant with the child that Tim and I had wanted. I didn't know for sure what I would do about it, but I knew the right thing to do was to go to Tim and see if things could be worked out between us. I went to Sweetwater and made a time to talk with Tim. He had moved back into our house by this time. I was going to see how his reaction would be before I told him about the pregnancy. We talked, and Tim showed no remorse for what he had done, so we both decided that this couldn't be fixed. I left with a feeling that nothing could fix what had already been broken, so I didn't mention the pregnancy to him.

I went to the doctor who had delivered my son for my first real appointment, and who of all people did I meet in the doctor's office? Jeffery. He was there with some type of a cold or something, and his mother was with him. We exchanged a few words, and he asked me if I was happy. I wanted to tell him everything, but I just couldn't. I did tell him that I was moving back to Sweetwater with my parents. I could see by the look in his eyes that he knew that Tim and I were no longer together, but he didn't say anything.

He said that he would call me sometime and maybe we could get together and talk where it would be more private. He told me that he now lived in Abilene, Texas, and had gotten his accounting degree, so he was keeping books for Borden's Dairy products. He seemed very nice and appeared to care about the mess I had certainly made in my life.

Jeffery called me two days later at my mom's house and asked if I could meet him. I told him that I could come to Abilene because I certainly did not want Tim knowing that I was meeting up with Jeffery. He was already out to get custody of my son, and I had no real proof of Tim and my "friend's" affair other than what Tim had admitted to and what I had seen.

I met with Jeffery at a Dairy Queen, and we talked for hours just catching up. It felt good to have something in my life that seemed familiar. Everything else certainly did not feel very familiar to me. I was back at home with my parents where I hadn't been for three years, and much worse than that, I was an adult who felt like she was living in a child's world. It felt good to be close to something familiar. I didn't tell Jeffery at first about my pregnancy. I didn't think it was anything I needed to share with him. After all, we were only friends at this point.

After about two weeks of talking to Jeffery—on the phone, mostly— he invited me to go out to eat with him at a Mexican restaurant that he had heard of in San Angelo. I accepted. I was very unfamiliar with

San Angelo, and as we drove into the town, I began to have some very bad cramps. I tried to hide the pain, but Jeffery knew something was wrong. It felt like a gush of water between my legs, and when I looked down, my jeans were covered in blood. That's when I told Jeffery about my pregnancy.

He saw a sign that said "Hospital," so he took that exit, and we ended up at Shannon Hospital emergency room. The doctor who saw me said he needed to get me to surgery right away because I was bleeding very badly. He said that I was losing the baby, and if he didn't operate right away, I could die. I remember as they started an IV on me that I asked the nurse if I had to do this. I begged her not to do this. I didn't want to lose my baby. I remember as they were taking me into surgery, she told me I didn't have to have this surgery; it was my choice. I don't remember anything else after that. I think they had given me some type of medication or something.

When I woke up, Jeffery was sitting beside my bed. He told me that he was sorry that I had lost my baby. I cried, and he tried to soothe me. He said he had called my mom and told her what was happening. She said for me not to worry about my son and that he was in good hands.

The hospital discharged me as soon as I could drink something and not throw up. I remember when I got back to my mom's, she was very sweet, but I am not sure that she realized how badly it hurt for me to lose the baby. I tried to keep my feelings to myself because my dad had been diagnosed with Alzheimer's disease, and she had her hands full.

Jeffery and I started seeing each other on a regular basis. It felt right. I was still married to Tim, but we were in the last stages of our divorce. I didn't have the money that Tim had to fight the battles in court that my attorney told me was going to happen. He said this could drag out for years. He told me it would cost thousands of dollars, and if I signed a joint custody agreement that it would work out best for my son. He told me that Tim would have joint time with me, and it would be equaled out. I hesitantly agreed. What I didn't understand was that Tim would get our son through the school year. It was too late to change it, and I felt that my attorney had sold me out. I did get the chance to tell him that years later. That's when I found out that the attorney I had used was an alcoholic.

Time moved on, and I kept seeing Jeffery. He seemed to have changed and matured. He was still a little self- centered, but I attributed that to him being a bachelor and not used to sharing. It was an amazing evening when he asked me to marry him. He told me that he had never gotten over the fact that he had lost me. I felt good again about myself. I felt at ease for the first time in months. I felt like this was where I belonged.

We married in November. It was a beautiful wedding, and my son was ring bearer. I really had not wanted a large wedding, but Jeffery thought it would be good because it was his first marriage. I had picked an old-fashioned lace dress that I wanted to wear, and Jeffery wanted me to wear a flowing dress with a hoop skirt and long veil. He picked out the dress and veil. He picked out my matron of honor, his best friend's wife. Although she had been one of my friends in the days that Jeffery and I dated in earlier years, I had not seen her until then since Jeffery and I had broken up. I felt a little uneasy, but I was pretty happy to be fitting in. Being a wife was all that I had really known, so I was doing something that would make me happy for a change.

Jeffery and I went to Dallas on our honeymoon to Six Flags. We both laughed and had a wonderful time. When we got back, the cycle of verbal abuse started with little things like when I would drop my keys, Jeffery would pick them up and say things like "Silly, what would you do without me? You can't even hold on to your keys!" As time went on, it progressed to "You are so stupid. You can't even hold on to your keys." Jeffery seemed angry. He didn't like being around my son and often called him Tim's son. I wasn't happy. Although I didn't recognize exactly what was happening, the verbal and mental abuse was beginning.

By this time, Jeffery had taken a job in Snyder with an oil company, and we had moved there. I was working at Cogdell Hospital on the floor with surgery patients when the nursing director came to me and told me that the ambulance contract needed to be renewed, and she felt I should try to get the contract. I went to the city hall meeting and was awarded the contract for the Ambulance Service. Jeffery was excited again, and it seemed like the abuse was going to stop. He was actually proud of me because before i had gotten the contract. Another man had run the ambulance service under the terms of Red Cross. I was bringing in Emergency Medical Services to Snyder for the first time in Snyder's history.

It was a very exciting time in my life. I hired two females and two males to make up the team of our crew. Things were going pretty well.

I had just found out that I was pregnant with my third baby. Although the timing wasn't the best, I was happy to be having another child. By now, my son was nearly five. Jeffery was having a hard time accepting him and said he reminded him too much of Tim. Jeffery told me very often that he did not like Tim.

At Thanksgiving that year, my ambulance crew and I decided to have our Thanksgiving dinner together, so we all cooked and made lunch. When we were ready to eat, I looked for Jeffery and my son. I found my son outside in the snow with his shoestrings tied together. My son told me that Jeffery had tied his shoes together. When I confronted Jeffery about it, he told me that my son had followed him outside and he didn't want him tagging along, so he tied his shoelaces together. After this, I would not allow Jeffery to be alone with my son.

When I became pregnant with our daughter, Jeffery's behaviors became worse. After he locked me in the apartment and spit in my face, I left him. By this time, I was starting early contractions because of the stress, and I feared for our baby's life as well. I filed charges on Jeffery for family violence, and his parents bailed him out of jail.

I found myself another apartment, and I came home to find him lying on the bed. He had gone to the landlord telling her he was my husband and I had forgotten to give him the key. During that time, people were not allowed to get a divorce if there was a pregnancy involved. There were no family violence shelters or sources of support for anyone going through what I was going through with him, and the Tracy Thurman law had not been put into place yet. I tried desperately to make things work with Jeffery, but in the end, I knew that it wouldn't and that he hadn't changed.

We were separated when my daughter was born. He told me that he would come to the hospital and take her from me if I didn't let him be there when she was born. The cycle of abuse works on the victim really well. It starts off small and moves up to bigger types of abuse until it has spiraled out of control. The thing the abuser has going for them is control. As long as they have power over the victim, they are winning., and I allowed Jeffery to take back the control by moving back in with him after my daughter and I came home from the hospital.

We moved back to Abilene after my daughter was born, and I went to work at Hendricks Hospital in the lab. To Jeffery, nothing that I did paid enough or was good enough. He constantly complained about our daughter being too noisy and nothing being the way he liked it in the house. He was very picky about the house being spotless, and he didn't want toys anywhere on the floor when he was at home.

The day I left him, he was in the drive threatening me. As I pulled out of the driveway, he latched on to the door, but I had locked it. I drove away, leaving him standing in the street threatening to come after me. I went to my mom and dad's house. My mom was out of town, and my dad told me that I could stay. I ran into an old friend from high school, and she told me that she had been looking for a roommate, so my daughter and I moved into her apartment.

Things were starting to look up for me. I found a job very quickly, and I found a wonderful childcare for my daughter. I worked ten-hour shifts four nights a week. I barely made ends meet, but God sent several angels in my direction. My roommate's mom would go to Dyess Air Base commissary and buy milk for about half the price I paid at the store, so my daughter always had milk. My mom and dad would help with diapers, and Jeffery's parents would help with medical bills. Jeffery did not help at all. He finally agreed to a divorce, and he did pay for that.

He had court ordered supervised visitation with our daughter because of his violent tendencies. He came once to see her, and he started trying to kiss me instead. When I told him that I didn't want anything to do with him, he started to slap me. I picked up a telephone and slammed it into his face, and then I told him that he had no more control over me, that I was no longer weak, and I would make him wish he was dead if he ever laid another hand on me or my children.

After that, I regained control over my life. Jeffery no longer was a threat to me. Timothy's affair with my "friend" didn't bother me or control my emotions anymore. I became strong for what I had been through. I realized that it is me and no one else who sets the course of my life. From there, I headed forward and took on the challenge. I no longer felt that I had to depend on anyone for anything other than myself. I knew that I would be okay and so would my children. Life was starting to be good again in Sweetwater, Texas, for me, my daughter, and my son.

Kerrie at ambulance contract signing when
EMS was brought to Snyder

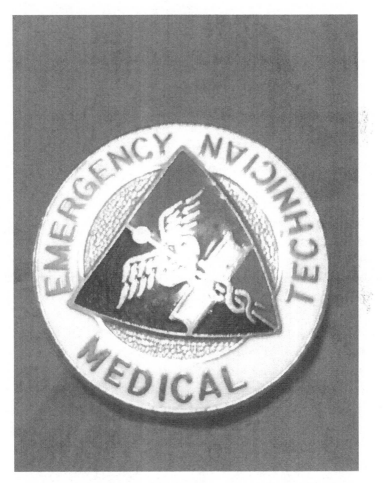

Emergency Medical Technician pin worn by Kerrie Bullard

Chapter 4

When my son was born, I was seventeen years old—really too young to become a mother, especially the mother of a baby who cried all of the time with colic. At thirteen years old, I began babysitting in the summers and on weekends. I loved taking care of children and having that responsibility. The babies were always sweet, and the older children were fun to play with.

The parents that I babysat for always bragged about how lucky they were to have me as a babysitter because not only did I take very good care of their children, I also enjoyed cleaning their house and doing laundry. To me, that was kind of like role-playing the lady of the house, and I found it a joy to do.

When I had my son, I found that being the mother and wife of the house was full time. When I babysat, it was just a few hours a day, and then I could go home and do whatever I wanted to do at home and be a child. I can remember those first few months of being a mother. It was emotionally, physically, and mentally draining. I cried a lot and cried along with my son when he cried with colic. I had never before not been able to soothe a baby when they cried, but here, this baby, my own child, didn't seem to be able to be soothed. I found myself wondering if he even liked me. I loved him and thought it should be an instant feeling that he would have love for me. I guess when he was born, I just expected him to give me back the love I tried to give him, and I didn't know that babies have to learn to love as they grow.

Babies are not giving when they are born; they are needy and have a need to be nurtured, so my thoughts on motherhood were totally wrong. I learned with time how to take care of a baby with colic and how to be a good wife as well. It was a lot for a seventeen-year-old to take in, but it was a responsibility that I made the choice to do, so I handled it.

After my son turned six months old, he was, for the most part, a very happy baby; and the best part: he was sleeping all night. It was amazing to me that this baby who had once cried all of the time, making me a nervous wreck, had become the best part of my life now.

As I think back to his first Christmas, I have to laugh because there were so many toys for him under that Christmas tree that it took two pictures to get them all in a photograph. It didn't seem that I could buy him enough that year. He wasn't really old enough to know what those gifts were, but that was part of the immaturity in me, that was me still basically being a child.

As my son grew older, it seemed that we became more distant from each other, especially after his dad and I divorced. It was almost as if we were strangers at times. But when he got into his teenage years, he began to have a greater need for me. I was thrilled at the thought that he could possibly be my little guy again. My love for him never stopped, but somehow it had just become somewhat estranged. I had to learn to accept what love he could give me and give him what love he would accept from me. I think he learned this from his father because, for the most part, he had stayed with his dad.

He seemed to be jealous of my daughter and even put one of my guns in her mouth once while I was at work. The gun was not loaded, but she did not know this. In earlier years, he had fed her car wax to see if she liked it, and he turned an iron on in her room, leaving it face down on the carpet. It almost seemed as if he were trying to harm her, or worse. I felt like I had to do something to intervene with these feelings, so I took him to a psychologist to have a psychological on him completed. The findings were that he had a very serious antisocial disorder and that he needed therapy to help him with these feelings of hatred and antisocial behaviors. As I tried to get help for him, his father fought me on this. He told my son that I was trying to make him look crazy, and he talked my son into going back to his house to live with him. Once again, his dad had betrayed me, and this time, he betrayed his son.

A year later, while I was at work at the sheriff's office, I received a telephone call from his dad. He told me that I had until 10:00 p.m. to pick my son up or my son would be living on the streets of Fort Worth, Texas. He told me that his current wife had awakened and found my son standing over her with a knife, and she didn't feel comfortable having him in her house. I immediately went to Fort Worth, Texas, and picked him and all of his belongings up and brought him home with me.

It was very apparent that he had a lot of anger issues as well as some personal problems he was dealing with. There were times that he would become so angry that he would roll his hand into a fist and put it in my face like he wanted to hit me. On one occasion, he put his fist in Charlie's face, and Charlie immediately put my son against the wall telling him if he wanted to fight, then the fight would be on; but if he had no intentions of carrying through with the threat, then to keep it to himself. That seemed to be the end of the fist thing. It seemed that he walked on the line of being in trouble with the law but just stayed clear of getting into trouble.

He was kind of a rebel child. He hung out with his best friend who was also kind of a rebel. When I look back, I think about the things they did, and really they weren't so bad, but there was a thin line between what they did and being law-abiding. I believe that they both wanted to have that kind of James Dean appearance. If I look at it that way, it seems like they were both kind of normal for their age.

Although it was against my advice, my son got married at a very young age. Although he was an adult and able to sign his own marriage license, I still urged him to wait and enjoy some of his life. But against my wishes, he married a seventeen-year-old girl who, by the time she was eighteen, became the mother of my first grandchild. My son joined the marines very early into their marriage. I begged him not to join the marines because I had seen others' sons who basically lost their personality after joining the marines. Their moms described them as being a different person after coming back from basic training. I urged my son to join the air force, army, or navy, but not the marines. However, once again, his dad intervened and got him to the enlistment office, and he joined the marines.

During the time that he was in basic training, I received a letter from him two or three times a week, begging me to get him out. There was nothing I could do for him because he was now the property of the United States armed forces. His wife stayed with her mom after he left for basic training. She found out that she was carrying their first child.

We had somewhat of a relationship but not as close as I wanted it to be. She had not gotten to know me very well, and it was understandable that she would not be as close to me as I wanted her to be. Her mom worked all of the time, and so did her dad. It wasn't until she went in labor with my first granddaughter that I learned how really beautiful this lady was inside and out. As she lay there in labor, I stroked her arm and rubbed her stomach. I cried with her when she cried and let her know that she was not alone.

My son was unable to get home right then because of his basic training, and her mom had not been able to get off of work until later in the day to be there with her. After twelve hours of labor, the doctor decided that she needed a cesarean section. I remember, that night as she was in surgery, I paced the hallway waiting to hear that she had given birth safely. My first granddaughter was born that night during an October thunderstorm. She was healthy, and my daughter-in-law was okay after the delivery.

Just when I thought I couldn't ask for more, I was asked by hospital staff if I could continue staying at the hospital to help my daughter-in-law. It was my pleasure. During that time, I was able to help care for my new granddaughter. This was one of the most precious gifts anyone could have ever given me. I remember calling my son's dad and telling him that he was a grandfather, and he smugly said, "Its granddad, not grandfather." What a hateful way to end such a beautiful day, I thought to myself. I didn't let it bother me, though. This was one of the most joyous occasions of our life.

I loved being a grandmother, and when my daughter-in-law left the hospital, I was unprepared for the heartbreak of watching my granddaughter in the car drive off to her mother's house where she would be thirty miles away. I know that doesn't seem very far but when you've been taking care of your first grandchild for several days around the clock, and all of a sudden, you're not, it may as well ne a million miles away.

I started going to get my granddaughter and keeping her at my house with me on the weekends to give my daughter-in-law some time to herself. I remembered how tough it was to be a young mother, having a child at a young age myself. I thought it would give me some quality time with my granddaughter as well. I enjoyed every minute that I had with this beautiful child. By the time my granddaughter was four months old, my son was stationed in Florida and out of basic training. He came to move his wife and child there with him. I didn't think I would ever feel such heartache as I did when they drove off with my little granddaughter.

I would see her toys at my house and cry. Her crib made me cry. And as I washed the last of her bottles, I really broke down. I didn't know what I would do with my weekends or how I would survive being away from her. My daughter-in-law knew and understood how I missed my granddaughter and would often call and put her on the phone. She would keep me updated on the new things my granddaughter was doing.

Although in my deepest of hearts I knew that this was the best thing for my daughter-in-law, son, and granddaughter, the selfish part of me often came out wishing they would come back home as I longed to see them all so badly. I got my wish just before my granddaughter turned a year old. They were back, and I had my granddaughter with me. It was the best feeling to feel her as she was in my arms and hear her little giggles. I had missed them all so.

My son was never the same. He tried hard, but he almost had no feelings left inside. He loved his wife and child, but something was missing. He and his wife fought often, sometimes becoming physical with each other. I remember, once, the police were called to their house, and the officer asked me if I had seen the pig sty they lived in.

My son complained that this was what caused their problems, and my daughter-in-law told me it was because my son didn't seem to have any inner feelings and was very cold toward her at times. I could see both sides of the story, but I didn't know what to do to help them. It must have been terrible for them both to have those kinds of feelings inside them where once they both shared happy, loving feelings.

I usually came to the defense of my daughter-in-law. I had seen her at her worst and most painful times and knew what she had gone through to get that baby girl here. I had grown to love her very deeply. I couldn't stand the thought of either of them hurting. I prayed for them and gave it to God because I had no control over this.

I kept my granddaughter every weekend and took her to church with me every Sunday. She loved going to Sunday school and became a big part of the church members' lives. My son eventually went to work as a jailer at the sheriff department. And during the time he was working there, my daughter-in-law and he separated. It broke my heart, but at least the fighting stopped. I continued to get my granddaughter every weekend, and on one Sunday, her mom came to me and told me she had been feeling very dizzy and sick. I took her to the emergency room, and that's when we found out that we were expecting a second grandchild.

I called my son and told him that he needed to speak with his wife. That is when they got back together. Seven months later, we had another beautiful baby girl.

This time around was a little different because my son was there when this child was born. He got to cut her umbilical cord and be the first to hold her. I remember, when I found out that my daughter-in-law was pregnant, I began immediately talking to the baby through the womb. I wanted her to know me when she arrived. Unlike the last time, the Caesarean was planned, and my daughter-in-law didn't have to go through quite as much as she did with the first delivery.

When I saw my second granddaughter for the first time, I began talking to her. I remember that she looked me up and down as if she were thinking, *There is that voice I've been hearing, and what is that it is coming from?* I continued keeping both grandchildren at my house on the weekends to give my son and my daughter-in-law some private time together. It was a good time for a while.

My daughter-in-law decided that she wanted to go to nursing school, so my son applied for a job in Lubbock, Texas, at the sheriff department and was hired. They moved to Levelland. It was a bittersweet time. I knew it could be a good move for them, but I also knew that there would be a distance between my granddaughters and me.

I'm not really sure what happened, but I think my son felt threatened by the fact that my daughter-in-law was succeeding at something in nursing school. He began accusing her of having affairs. On the advice of his father, one day when my daughter-in-law came home, pretty much everything, including food, was removed from the house—my son had moved out. I remember that I was on my way to Wednesday evening services at church when I received the call from my daughter-in-law. She was crying so hard that I could barely understand her. When she told me what had happened, I was in disbelief. We both cried together, and I told her that I needed to get some money to her because she said she only had one dollar, no food, and no gas. I wired her money that night, and I told her where to go to get some help with food. She was able to make things work and complete nursing school.

I was so proud the day she graduated from nursing school. I am still angered by the way my son left, and by the advice he was given by his father. Despite the problems he and my daughter-in-law had, those children, nor my daughter in law for that fact, should have ever been left in that situation. As for my son's dad, he had no business getting involved in their business and providing my son with that kind of advice.

My granddaughters and I have talked about that night on many occasions, and I have listened as my oldest granddaughter told me about seeing her mom cry and her feeling terrified because their home life as they knew it was gone.

As the end of their marriage grew near, I did everything I could to try and be there for my daughter-in-law and my grandchildren. I did not want to ever lose that relationship. My son, on the other hand, did well for the first few years after the divorce as far as seeing his children and paying his child support; but as time went by, I believe he became depressed. He lost his job at the sheriff department and stopped paying child support. He basically lost everything and moved back to Sweetwater where he began living in my parents' old house.

He tried to live with his father, but his father was very demanding and controlling. His father took every opportunity to put him down and make him feel worthless. My son's health began to decline. The best advice I could offer my son was to move back to Sweetwater and get somewhere where he did not have to be belittled and controlled, somewhere where he would have family support and love, so that was when he chose to move back to Sweetwater.

Through the years, I have tried to understand exactly why life has been so difficult for my son, but I guess he has chosen his own route in some sense. I can't help but go back to the day when I tried to talk him out of joining the marines. In my heart of hearts, I believe they took away his personality, and it never really came back. Along with the fact that he already had some mental health issues going on, stemming back to when I took him for the psychological, I believe he just got lost.

Today, his daughters do not have a lot to do with him. The oldest granddaughter calls him, and sends him texts. My daughter-in-law has remarried and lives in somewhat of a chaotic lifestyle. But in the presence of all of that, my granddaughters have turned out to be very smart, talented young ladies. As for the relationship that I had with my daughter-in-law, I still love her with all of my heart, and I am thankful that she came into my life. Most of all, I am proud that she is the mother of my granddaughters. For without her love and guidance, I do not believe they would have become who they are today.

My son has always taken the stance that everything that happens to him is someone else's fault. He never takes the blame for his faults. His dad continues to send off confusing signals. Sometimes he acts like a father should, and sometimes he becomes controlling and mean especially when he sees things are not perfect in my son's world. I just try to love my son the best I can, and I pray daily that his world will get better. I pray that he will find peace within himself and that he will learn to love unconditionally and learn that everything that happens is not someone else's fault. I pray for his health to get better. He has had so many health issues, and I know if he could find healing in his body, he would find healing in himself.

Sometimes I find myself taking the blame for his behaviors, thinking that if I had been older and more mature when he was born that maybe his life would have been different. And sometimes I think if his dad would have been better at parenting, things may have been different for him. My son has told me many times that he would love to hear the words "I'm proud of you, son" from his dad. I don't know if that will ever happen because I believe that his dad will never be content that anyone besides himself is good at anything.

I still maintain somewhat of a relationship with my daughter-in-law. Although she is no longer married to my son, she will always be my daughter-in-law. I have told her this. My granddaughters and I still visit as often as we can. I miss them dearly when they are not here. They are now in their teen years and have many things going on in life.

I recently told them that there is a time in your life when all you want to do is be with your grandparents, and then there's the time when you outgrow them and have other interests. I explained that although they are reaching the points in their life where their other interests will seem to be the most important thing in their life to them, the yearning to be with their grandparents will come back around again. I explained to them that although it seems like they will have an eternity to spend with those they love, time does not stand still, and time moves quickly the older we get. I asked them to think about this and not let more time than they really have pass by before they find the time to spend with their grandparents again. We all have different seasons in our lives, and it is how we choose to live in those seasons that will determine the memories that remain in our life.

Kerrie at age 17 just before she married

Chapter 5

After divorcing Jeffery and having some freedom from the abuse, I became more independent and enjoyed life much more than I ever had. For the first time in my life, I was single, living on my own, and did not depend on anyone other than myself to take care of me and my daughter.

By this time, my son was living with his father; and even though Timothy had done what he had done, I had chosen to forgive him and get along with him the best that I could for my son's sake. Jeffery, on the other hand, was another story. I still had some healing to do with that one.

Lola was one of my dearest friends from back in my junior high school years. We had become very close and practically lived together throughout junior high. She understood what I had gone through, probably more than anyone because she had gotten married just after her eighth grade year, so she knew what it was like to be a child bride. The only difference was that Lola had no children.

Lola played a very important part of my life again during this time. She called me one night and invited me to go to a dance with her and her husband. She told me there was someone there that she wanted me to meet named Charlie. She said he worked with her husband and he played in the band. She said that she felt because of his musical interest, we might have a lot in common.

I was very tired because I had just returned from Austin as I had been to a special Olympic outing with some of the clients that I worked with, but I decided to go. I will never forget what went through my mind as I entered the door of the local VFW and Lola pointed out

Charlie to me. There stood this man with a beard nearly to his waist and hair that came to his waist. As I turned around to leave, Lola told me that I shouldn't judge him by his appearance. I just responded to her that he looked like someone who could be using drugs, and that I didn't need that because I didn't use drugs and my daughter didn't need to be around that.

I can remember Lola laughing and telling me that looks can be deceiving and I should at least meet him. Not wanting to cause a scene, I reluctantly agreed. This was really the first time that I had been in a bar. It was something different for me, but the music was really good. The band took a break, and I met Charlie Blair for the first time. Charlie was very soft-spoken and had a laugh that would fill the room. He played bass guitar and sang almost with a whisper, and I would later learn that some called him Whispering Bill' after Bill Anderson because of his soft voice.

The first time we met, we talked for about fifteen minutes, and then he returned to the stage with the band to play. He told me to listen for the first song because it would be played especially for me. It was "Sensuous Woman." I still to this day cannot listen that song without thinking of Charlie up there on the stage singing it. My friend and I left before the dance was over, and I didn't talk to Charlie again for a while.

As luck would have it, I met him at the courthouse accidentally. He was coming out as I was going in. The thought of him being a drugee was in the back of my mind as I spoke to him. He told me not to think badly of him being there because he had gone voluntarily to raise the amount of child support he was paying on a child he had with another woman. He asked if I could meet him at the café for coffee, and I told him I would as soon as I had concluded my business there.

A short time before I met Charlie, someone had broken into my car and had stolen a box of checks. These thieves had gone all over town writing checks on my name and cashing them at the local convenience stores, telling the cashiers that they were mowing lawns for me and were cashing their checks. Local police had captured the culprits who turned out to be thirteen-year-old boys. I had to go in and identify my checks so they could proceed with prosecution on them. They certainly were my checks, and they were placed on probation for stealing my checks. They were ordered to pay restitution but never did.

After I left court, I met up with Charlie at Al's Café. We had coffee and made plans to go out the following night on our first date. Charlie told me that he had been divorced for ten years and had a twelve-year-old daughter. He said he had not seen his daughter in a long time because she lived in New Mexico and his ex would not let her come to Texas to see him. There was a lot of casual conversation before we left the café.

I remember the first date that Charlie and I had, but I don't remember many in between that and the time we got married. We often just went to a café in town at night, had dinner, and just talked. We both seemed to have a lot to talk about. My daughter was not very trusting of men. In fact, she really didn't like men very much and rarely had anything to do with men unless it was her grandfather's. But when she met Charlie, she ran to him, jumped on his lap, and began pulling on his beard. Charlie filled the room with his laughter; and for my daughter, it was love at first sight with him.

Charlie and I married on March 29, 1982, in a very casual ceremony. We had a reception at the VFW, and there were a lot of the usual VFW dancers there. That began twenty-three years of happiness for me, my children, Charlie's daughter, and Charlie. After Charlie and I married, his daughter who was twelve now started coming to visit with us on a regular basis. I was twenty-three, so having her there with us was like having a good friend there for me. I could relate well with her, and she and I had many good times.

Charlie was quite a bit older than me, fourteen years to be exact, but that didn't matter to me. Charlie was very supportive in everything I did. He told me that he thought I should stay home with my daughter at least until she started school, so I did. My son loved Charlie. He liked just being around him, and Charlie loved my son in return. Charlie was a diesel mechanic and drove a wrecker for eighteen wheelers. The kids loved getting to ride with him in the wrecker.

When my daughter began kindergarten, I began to pursue my career in law enforcement. I was accepted into the West Central Texas Council of Governments Law Enforcement Academy. Growing up in the small neighborhood that I did, one of my best friend's mom was a cop—the first lady cop in Sweetwater. I always admired her and wanted to be a cop just like her. I would see her coming and going from their house in her uniform and think to myself, *That could be me*. She gave me promise in becoming a cop.

I was excited when I was accepted into the academy because in those days, not many women were accepted into the academy, unlike today. There were two other women in my class. The three of us actually graduated at the top of the class. While I attended the police academy, I was living out another dream. I had started singing with Charlie's band and playing the keyboards in another band. Life was good.

Charlie and I had so many things in common, and we had a good family life at home. The kids loved him, he loved them, and he loved me as much as I loved him. I was extremely happy. Charlie and I traveled a lot with the band on the weekends and opened for some top country music stars. The money was good, and we had fun. It was as exciting as it was fun. Charlie had played at the original Gilley's bar in Pasadena, Texas, before we met. He had lived in the Houston area before returning to Sweetwater to take care of his mom who was sick. It was exciting just knowing someone that had been a part of such a historic place where the movie *Urban Cowboy* had been filmed. While playing at Gilley's, he played for people like Mickey Gilley and Johnny Lee. He knew people like Charlie Daniels. To me, this was exciting. Charlie had a lot of talent and was one of the best bassists that I had ever met.

Time moved on, and I graduated from the police academy. I remember going to the Nolan County Sheriff Department in November 1985 and applying for a job as a night deputy. The lady who handed me the application told me that whoever was hired would need to be a commissioned officer, and when I told her that I was commissioned, I could tell that she took an interest.

When I got home, my phone was ringing—it was the sheriff department calling me to ask me to come back for an interview. I went back and was immediately hired. I was to report the next day. Everything happened so fast. They took me down, and I was sworn in as a deputy. They gave me a badge and uniforms. I was living my dream. I was now a cop. I was so excited to begin my career.

Charlie was really supportive. He watched my daughter at night while I worked. He always told me that he knew when he married me that I had children and that they were a part of the package! Charlie and I had bought our first house by now, and we loved living where we did. The little house was out of the city limits but close enough to town that we could easily drive in to get what we needed. I took a correspondence course and got my jailer's license because it was required by the sheriff department.

Sometimes, when we booked inmates into the jail, the sheriff would make a special appearance into the booking area and say that he would escort the inmate into the jail. The jail was located on the second floor, and there was an elevator going up to the jail. There were times when I could hear bumping noises coming from the elevator, and when I would ask the jailer about it, she would just say that it was nothing. I later found out that the sheriff was stopping the elevator and hitting the inmates. I didn't find this out until after I left that sheriff department in Nolan County.

On April 19, 1986, a tornado hit Sweetwater, Texas. I was at home when it hit, but I knew something was going to happen with the weather because the clouds looked as if they were pushing at each other and the electricity was going on and off. My mom and dad came to the house and informed me that a tornado had hit town and that there was a lot of damage and devastation. The phones weren't working, but for some reason, my phone worked for just a minute, long enough for my daughter to call me from her grandmother's house in Roby, Texas, and for me to let her know that I was okay.

She had spent the weekend with her grandparents in Roby, Texas, so she was safe; and by now my son and his dad had moved to Fort Worth, Texas, and he was safe. I immediately went in to the sheriff department and partnered up with another deputy, and we began the task of checking neighborhoods for injuries. There were three children that had not yet been accounted for, but we later found them. And they were safe and unharmed.

I had never seen anything like what I was witnessing. Places where houses had stood were now empty lots. There was no house there. It was if the house never existed. People were walking around dazed. There was only one life lost in that tornado. Because of the damage and devastation from that tornado, there could have been so many more lives lost. As I drove through the old neighborhood where I grew up, it was sometimes hard to tell where I was because the landmarks I used to know were now gone. It was like being in a strange neighborhood.

Today, as I drive through there, I still see some vacant lots with a sidewalk leading up to where a house had once stood—a reminder of that day; a reminder to be thankful for those that made it through it without harm or injury; a reminder to always be mindful that we have no control over what can happen with the weather at any given moment.

I cannot fathom what the family who had a loss must have gone through. It had to be very tragic for them. Although there were many injuries, the footprints of that day will forever be engraved in the hearts and minds of those of us who were there. Things at the Nolan County Sheriff Department seemed to be taking some strange turns. Other deputies were talking about the walls having ears. Inmates were filing complaints against the sheriff, and I had a strange feeling that this is not a place that I wanted to be. I've always been taught that the one thing you have in this world that does not cost you anything is your reputation, and that is something that you should never lose.

In November 1986, I met Sheriff Mickey Counts, who offered me a job at the Fisher County Sheriff Department. I made my decision to leave Nolan County and go to work for Fisher County Sheriff Department. The day after I left Nolan County Sheriff Department, there was a jail break. It seemed the jailer on duty during the day had not completed a headcount of the prisoners when they were returned from the gym, and several had climbed up on the top of the jail tank to hide until the next shift started. Because I had left, there was an inexperienced deputy who took my shift. He did not know to do a beginning of shift headcount of the inmates with the jailer who was leaving, and she left without doing this. As he walked down the halls to administer medications, the inmates on top of the jail tank jumped him and took him hostage.

I later learned that they thought it would be me relieving the other jailer and had planned on jumping both of us, since we were both females, and taking us both as hostages. But since she didn't do a headcount, she escaped getting taken hostage, and I escaped as well. Unfortunately, another deputy had to pay the price for another's mistakes. Fortunately, he escaped without injury, and the inmates were taken back into custody after somewhat of a standoff. Just another reminder of how God's hand can be protective when you don't even realize it.

Not long after I left Nolan County, the sheriff was indicted on federal charges and served time in federal prison. I felt good about my decision to leave Nolan County when I did. I began my career in Fisher County as the first commissioned female deputy in the county and the first female to patrol the county. My first shift on patrol alone was a midnight shift. It was Christmas Eve, and I received a call to the little community of Hobbs, Texas. The dispatcher told me that he could not understand the caller very well because she spoke a lot of Spanish and not much English. He told me to let him know if I needed backup.

I arrived at a house located in the middle of a cotton field. It was pitch-black out there, and I was thankful to have a long mag flashlight. As I checked out the house, the dispatcher did not answer me when I called. I called to him several times; meanwhile I could also hear a disturbance inside the house. It sounded like some glass breaking. I asked him to send backup, and he still did not respond. I reluctantly got out of the car and made my way to the house. My heart was throbbing inside my throat. This was what I had trained for all of those weeks in the academy, but I was breaking a rule—I had no backup in a dangerous situation.

I knocked on the door and announced myself. A young Spanish woman opened the door. She had a bloody nose, a black eye, and she was crying. She could not speak English, and there was a very strong odor of alcohol coming from the house. I could see several men inside but no other women. She told me in fragmented English that she was the only women there and that she had been the target of domestic violence from her husband. I got her into the car with me, and I radioed the sheriff department again for backup but got no answer.

In those days, there were no cell phones, and the only contact I had was with radio. I left with the woman in the car with me and took her to the emergency room at the hospital. From there, I called the sheriff at home and explained to him what was going on. He went to the dispatch office and found the dispatcher asleep. When he and I went back to that residence, everyone was gone. We called the family violence shelter and got a place for the woman to stay. Her injuries were not life-threatening. I developed a very long time friendship with this woman and still call her my friend today.

She was able to get some legal help through Crime Victims funding. She got her education, learned to speak English well, and opened a daycare in another town. Being a victim of family violence, I felt very connected to her and to the newly opened Family Violence Shelter. As for the dispatcher, he was no longer allowed to dispatch and ended up working for the road crew. I became good friends with the director of the Family Violence shelter and got to serve ten years on their board of directors.

Things were great with working in Fisher County. The kids called me Lady Blue. It was meant as a compliment because at the time, there was a television series on named *Lady Blue*, and it was about a female cop who always solved her cases. I felt at home in Fisher County, and my family was settling in there as well. My daughter was now in the fourth grade, and my son was a freshman. We bought a house in Rotan, Texas, and we sold our little house in Sweetwater very quickly. Charlie found a job in a diesel shop in Rotan, and we loved life there.

Kerrie's Daughter as a Cheerleader at school

Chapter 6

Charlie Blair was the love of my life. He was everything a woman could ever ask for in a husband: funny, talented, handsome, sweet, thoughtful, and loving. The night I met Charlie, I thought that he probably was not anyone I would want to be associated with. He kind of looked like he wasn't the family type. His hair came to his waist, and his beard came down to his waist.

The first time I saw him, he was playing his bass guitar on stage. It was a chance meeting. We were introduced by mutual friends. When I saw him, I wanted to leave, but my friend persuaded me to stay and meet him. Five minutes into meeting him, we were talking and laughing like we had known each other for a long time. He was so easy to talk to. And when I was talking, he listened. That was the beginning of a twenty-three-year marriage, friendship, and time that I wish I could have made just stand still.

We married on March 29, 1982. It wasn't a formal wedding; we wore matching western shirts and pants, and there was a dance afterward at the local VFW where Charlie and his band played. Then off to a honeymoon in East Texas—the beginning of many ups and downs but mostly happy times.

Charlie worked as a diesel mechanic during the week and, on Saturday nights, played for local dances. Before meeting me, Charlie had lived in Houston, Texas, and played at the well-known Gilley's Club with stars like Mickey Gilley, Johnny Lee, and Charlie Daniels. We both loved music and enjoyed writing songs together. Although Charlie had never taken any kind of music lessons, he could play; and at any given moment, he could tell me what notes I was playing on the piano. He had a perfect pitch for music.

When I would travel and get lost, I could call Charlie and describe what was around me, and he could get me on track. I often wondered how Charlie became so smart. Once, when my daughter was outside playing with a friend who's bike was broken, I overheard her telling her friend, "Charlie can fix it. He can fix anything." She was pretty much right there.

Charlie and I bought our first house on Ponderosa Drive in Sweetwater about a year after we married. It wasn't a real fancy house, but I had everything we needed. We loved it in that little neighborhood. It was on the outskirts of town, just far enough out to be in the county but close enough to town that it didn't take a minute to drive in to the store. There was a small clique of houses in the neighborhood, and the kids would all ride their bikes in the evening up and down the street. We had a male Doberman who stayed right behind the kids, making sure they were protected from anything that might go wrong.

It was a good time in life for us. I was beginning my career in law enforcement, my daughter was starting school, and Charlie worked less than a mile from where we lived. Charlie had just gotten a promotion at his shop and was now shop foreman and took on the task of driving the big wrecker that picked up trucks. He and I both had our respective places in the community and felt good with our lives. I worked nights, and Charlie took care of the kids while I was at work. Most of the time, my son chose to be with his biological father, so my daughter was all that we had for the most part. When he would be called out for a wrecker call at night, he would just take my daughter with him and put her in the sleeper. She was such a sound sleeper; she never remembered going out with him.

Charlie loved kids and gave many of the neighborhood children a ride in the big wrecker. I remember once when my sister was living in Vermont, she and her family came down, and Charlie took them for a ride in the wrecker. They beamed with joy as he allowed them to pull the big air horn. It was a happy time for all, and I beamed with joy knowing that my husband was able to bring this much happiness to some with such a small gesture. Making the decision to sell our little house on Ponderosa Drive was a hard choice, but in order to go to work for Fisher County as a deputy sheriff, we really didn't have much of a choice. We sold the little house and bought a house in town in Rotan.

Charlie was about ready for a career change and accepted a job at a truck repair shop in Rotan, and things were working out very well for us. By now, my daughter was in the third grade, so the move was hard for her. But she adapted very easily because she had the type of personality that poured into another's soul, and the children there took an instant liking to her, which is hard for some in a small town. Getting used to living inside the city limits was the hard part because we had lived in the country for so long. There were noises we were not used to, such as people walking the streets at all hours, cars and trucks going by, and just having a neighbor so close that they seemed to know all of our business. Now we had to lock our doors because everyone knew if we were at home or not, and the probability of a burglary was a high risk if the doors weren't locked.

Times were changing for us. The children were getting older. By now, my son was a freshman in high school and had moved in with us. He didn't have as much of an easy time moving into the small-town life as my daughter. He had been living with his father who now lived in North Richland Hills near Dallas, Texas. Small-town life was a hard cup of tea for him to swallow. The kids dressed differently than he did. He was used to wearing dressy clothing, and Rotan kiddos dressed in jeans and T-shirts. My son just had to learn to adjust. Once he met his best friend, he became more comfortable with the small town ways, but it took a few arguments and a lot of stress on his part. Charlie and I tried as much as we could to help, but sometimes things are just better left alone; and in this case, this is what we had to do. My son was a little on the hard-headed side and didn't like to listen a lot to anything, which meant he was a typical teenager!

By now, we had bought a place in the country, so life seemed to be back to normal for us. We had 165 acres just out of town, far enough to be in the county but close enough to town to run into the store if something was needed. We felt so at home, almost like we were back on Ponderosa Drive where we had so many happy times.

Despite the hard-headedness, my son graduated from high school and joined the marines. But before he joined the marines, he married a young girl. My daughter, on the other hand, continued to progress, became a cheer leader, and excelled in sports throughout her junior and high school years. It was a bittersweet time for Charlie and me because the last one of our kids was leaving home.

By now, I had buried myself in college because I made a vow to get my degree. It's funny how it worked out. My daughter and I were both seniors the same year—she in high school and me in college. I graduated in December 1999, and she graduated in May 2000. Although she graduated, she continued to live at home. She didn't turn eighteen until July.

By now, my daughter had decided that she should be able to make her own choices. She was hanging out with different people that I didn't know, and sometimes she wouldn't come home until two or three in the morning. Although Charlie and I tried hard to let her be an adult, we couldn't just let her make bad choices. Charlie was driving a truck now and was on the road a lot, so he wasn't at home a lot to help. My daughter was going through something because at times she became abusive to me both verbally and physically. My heart was breaking very quickly because this is not how we had raised her to be.

We no longer played in bands or went to dances. We had outgrown this and just lived a normal life. I had become very involved in my church and now played the piano for the services and sang solos all of the time at church. My son had gotten married, and I now had a beautiful granddaughter whom I absolutely adored. On the very day that my daughter turned eighteen, she had one of her tantrums. She barreled down the hall calling me names, charging at me. These things all happened just in time for Charlie to walk in and see for himself. I could tell by the look on his face that he was in disbelief at what was coming out of her mouth. It was almost as if it was someone else's child, but once he heard for himself how she was talking to me and how near-violent she became, he told her to get her things and leave.

On her birthdays in the past, there had always been a big party and usually an expensive gift or a large amount of money for her to buy what she wanted. But on this particular birthday, before she left, I gave her a picture, not very expensive but of a very beautiful place. I told her it reminded me of the beautiful heart and spirit that she had once had. I told her when she looked at the picture to know that this is the beauty that I had always seen in her. I gave her a quarter in her card and told her to keep it close by and to use it to call me if she ever needed me. I believe this was one of the most heartbreaking times in my life. Letting go of my baby girl was so very hard. This was the child that had always been mine from the very start, and now she was going to be somewhere else. Not in my house but in another house. I cried as she drove out of the drive.

Dinner time was the worst time. Where there had once been laughter and conversations at the table, now there was just silence. Every day, I lived to get a phone call from her to hear her voice and know that she was okay. If I didn't hear from her, I wouldn't sleep until I did. The days seemed long. She had moved to the Dallas area with a boyfriend. I was so saddened because this is not the way she had been brought up. Our religious beliefs were totally different. This boy was a Jehovah's Witness. Obviously, he didn't have the Christian beliefs that we had.

One of the things that I had always done was take my children to church and make sure they knew who God was and how God wanted them to live. I prayed often for God to intervene and bring my daughter back to the life she was raised to live. One day, I received a phone call from my daughter. Although it was something that broke my heart and was hard to hear, it was also music to my ears. The boy she had been with was abusive to her, and she wanted to come home. I had to hold my composure, but I stayed with everything Charlie and I had told her in the past. I told her that she was welcome to come home and live with us, but there were rules that she would have to follow.

To have her back home with me was the best of feelings, to know that she was safe and to know that she was still my baby girl although she was eighteen years old now. The emptiness that I had felt in the past weeks was now gone and replaced by a feeling of knowing that my girl was back.

Kerrie as a Fisher County deputy

Fisher County Sleeve Patch worn by Deputy Kerrie Blair

Fisher County Badge worn by Deputy Kerrie Blair

Fisher County Badge worn by Deputy Kerrie Blair

Deputy Blair's DARE sleeve patch

Nolan County badge worn by Deputy Kerrie Blair

Nolan County sleeve patch worn by Deputy Kerrie Blair

Chapter 7

Time moved on sometimes in slow motion and sometimes too quickly. But we were happy with our life in Fisher County. When I first decided to go into the field of law enforcement, I really had a goal of helping children and families, so as I moved forward in my career, I worked a lot on sexual abuse, child abuse, and family violence calls.

I became very familiar with many of the stories that people would tell me about their family violence situation. I could sympathize with them because I had once been in their situation, but it seemed that I was always defending the victim to my fellow officers. The most common sentences that I would hear coming from their mouth was "I really can't sympathize with that woman because she keeps going back to him." I found myself often providing them with statistical information that in most cases, a victim will return to their abusive partner three to seven times before leaving for good, or being killed.

I would often remind them that while the percentage of reported male victims was small, there were also male victims as well as female victims. The reason for the small percentage of male victims was attributed to the fact that most male victims were too ashamed to report such violent episodes with their spouse. The unfortunate thing about family violence crime is that it is one of the most deadly crimes in small rural areas. The crime itself is not only dangerous to the victim; it is dangerous for other family members living in the home as well as the police officer who may respond to the call.

I remember early one morning receiving a call from dispatch that there was a structure fire on Highway 70 south of Roby nearly into Nolan County. I won't forget the words of the dispatcher as he told me that there may still be victims inside the home to include three children. Upon arrival at the scene, I saw a house totally engulfed in flames with no way of getting into the home. I knew if anyone was inside the home, they were more than likely deceased.

I was greeted at the scene by the Sweetwater chief of police. He told me to whom the home belonged to, and I had to keep my composure because the owner of the home was a woman that I had grown up with from first grade through adulthood. I had played soft ball with her. My children had played in the dugout with her beautiful children. I had to put this feeling of loss on my shoulder and deal with it later.

I noticed parked near the road people who I found out were her parents who lived on the adjacent property to hers. I spoke with them to find out that there were three children, and the mother of the children in the home to their knowledge. Her fourth child was in the car with the grandparents because she had spent the night with them, so she was accounted for. He parents informed me that the electricity to her home had been cut off, and she had been heating the home with a kerosene-type heater. They both also informed me that she had been in a relationship with a very violent paramour and that she had argued with him earlier in the evening according to the child who was in the car with them.

I spoke to the person who had reported the fire. He said he was in route to his workplace and saw the whiskey barrels on the front porch of the home blazing. He said although the house seemed to be fully involved in the fire, he ran around the house calling out for anyone but couldn't hear anything. He said he couldn't get to the front door because the concrete porch was burning. He told me it was as if something had been poured on that porch because of the concrete burning like it was. He said when he ran around to the back and attempted to push through the back door, it seemed like there was something against it, keeping it from opening. He said he could feel the heat even through the door.

Once the fire had been put out, I walked through the charred remains of the home. I was able to assess that there had in fact been a kerosene heater in the living room area of the home. I located it; it was intact. Based on the damage and heat from the fire, my original thought was that the heater probably would not have been recognizable had it have been the cause of the fire. But it was actually in good shape and was taken into evidence. I didn't believe it to be the culprit of the fire's origin.

Another thing I noticed was that the refrigerator had been moved into a position where it was blocking passage to the back door, and this is why entry was unable to be gained through the back door by the gentleman who discovered the fire. To the left of the living room was a master bedroom. In the doorway of that master bedroom, I discovered the body of the first child. She was lying facedown. Her face was still intact although the rest of her body was burned beyond recognition. The concrete flooring must have protected her face, although it was as if the skin of her face had shrunken down to about a third of its original size.

To the right of the living room was another bedroom, and that is where I discovered the other three bodies. The mother of the children had sat down on the bottom bed of the bunk beds, perhaps overcome from the smoke; she had fallen backwards. The younger two children's bodies were found under the bed frame huddled together. My thought was that their last thought in this life must have been thoughts of horror as they watched smoke and flames lapping at them. The beautiful children who had once played in the dugout with my children were now just charred remains, and their mother who always was seen with a smile and was surrounded by her radiant beauty was now charred muscle and bones in a crumpled-up heap.

From the evidence I had seen, I gathered that possibly someone had come to the home and got into an argument with the mom. The children, frightened by the arguing, were in their room hiding. Maybe the mom was knocked unconscious and placed on the bed in the children's room, or maybe she went in there to console them. The house was set on fire. The children couldn't get out because of the fire and smoke. The oldest child may have gone into her mom's room hoping for a way out or hoping to find her mom and was overcome by smoke in the doorway, collapsing and eventually burning to death.

Another scenario I came up with was that possibly the mom had been knocked unconscious in the front part of the house while in an argument with someone. The children were hiding in the back part of the home, afraid. The attacker set the home on fire, shoving the refrigerator up against the back door so that no one could gain entry or get out. He left through the front door, pouring the accelerant on the porch area so that no one could get out through that door. The mom regained consciousness and, looking for her children, may have heard them, headed for the area of their bedroom and eventually collapsed on their bed while they hid underneath the beds. I feel that in the confusion of everything, the oldest of the children attempted to find her mother— as maybe that is the last place she had heard her—and ended up in the doorway of the master bedroom, overcome by smoke.

Although the state fire marshall's office was unable to find any accelerant on the porch of the home, something caused the concrete to burn. They ruled that since no accelerant was found, the fire was possibly set by the kerosene heater. The bodies were in such a state of decomposition from the fire that there was not much information to gain from the autopsies.

I interviewed several people who were either ex-wives or ex-paramours of the violent paramour that the mother of the children was seeing at the time of the fire. I was told that he was very violent and that, while seeing him, he had made threats on their lives. One of the ladies who had been married to him before told me that he was so violent that while she was carrying their child, he beat her so badly that he fractured the collar bone of the fetus she carried. I found that he had beaten his own grandmother and broken her arm during the process, but she did not file charges on him. And when I interviewed his grandparents, they were so fearful of him that they refused to provide written statements because of the terror that he had put them through while he lived with them.

I continued to work on the case for years afterward, trying to get a shred of something that would be enough to get this man indicted for the murders of the woman and her children. By this time, he was doing penitentiary time for almost beating another woman to death in a bar with a pool cue. I spoke with people who had been associated with him throughout his life and people who had been associated with him after the death of this mother and her children. I was given statements by at least three women who said he told them that he had gotten by with killing before, and if they did not do as he said, he would get by with it again. They stated that this was during a process of one of his violent episodes of beating them.

I took the evidence that I had gathered through the years to the district attorney and was told that they were working on some things to try to get him indicted. To this day, the man has never been indicted; however, he is back in the penitentiary, serving the rest of his life there due to parole violations.

Even with that, I do not have peace of mind. I believe that he should have been prosecuted for the crime of murdering the children and their mother as I will always believe that he used an accelerant of some kind that was not detected by the state fire marshall's office and he murdered that mother and her children. The place where the house stood stayed an empty lot with reminders of what had been a home to some children who lost their lives in a very twisted fateful time of their mother's life. I knew that their last moments of life were more than likely pure agony. I knew at this time I had to do something to help children.

The only one who knows how the accounts of that evening really went down is the man who lives with this. I questioned our judicial system that with years of evidence I had gathered, nothing was done to atone for this crime. Maybe they felt that settling for whatever they could get for in other crimes was the best and easiest way out for them. Who really knows?

I do believe that there will come a day when he will have to answer for what he has done, and then he will be held accountable even if it's not on this earth. I look forward to that day. I hope at that time, I can maybe glance across heaven's floor and see this mother and her children as they embrace the fact that their murderer has finally been held accountable, and he will have to pay for what he has done.

Chapter 8

Although I loved living and working in Fisher County, I also knew that I wanted to help children in some way. I went to the sheriff and asked if it would be possible for me to get a day shift so that I could go to college and get a degree. I remember him telling me that he would always support me in anything that would ensure my education and would allow me to move forward.

I took this opportunity and enrolled in classes at Wayland Baptist University to begin the task of getting my bachelor's degree. The university itself was located in Lubbock, Texas, so the daily drive was two hours going there and two hours going back home. I went to classes from 6:00 p.m. until 10:00 p.m. It was a long road, but with the support of Charlie and my family, I was able to graduate in December 1999.

My daughter was a senior in high school. I always joked about us both being seniors the same year! Not to mention my first grandchild also attended my graduation. I don't think there are very many people who can say that their grandchild attended their college graduation and their daughter is a senior at the same time they are a senior! My granddaughter was just over a year old, but she attended.

In November 2000, I began my career with Child Protective Services as an investigator. I thought that I had finally found the job where God wanted me to be, the place where I would be able to help children and families. It was a hard transition at first because I had to go from looking at the abuse from the standpoint of a peace officer to looking at it in civil terms. I often found myself in the field trying to make a criminal case against people and had to be reminded that I needed to come over to the CPS side of things.

Through the years, I saw many things, but none worse than the death of a child caused at the hands of a parent. I will never forget the morning when I was headed off to work and I received a phone call from my supervisor telling me there had been a reported child death in one of the counties where I worked, and she wanted me to handle it.

Just like in the police academy, in the CPS academy, you train for things; but when the reality appears, you begin to question yourself if you are really ready for this. This was not the first child death that I had worked before, but it was different than most. The child had bruises from head to toe. She appeared to be very malnourished, but her sibling didn't have any appearance of abuse on her. The mom kept telling me that the deceased child was a diabetic. She was two-and-a-half years old and when I asked to walk through the house. The first thing I noticed was two Easter baskets full of candy. The dining room table had plates with cake in them. And when I observed the contents of the refrigerator, I observed that it was full of things that a diabetic should not have.

The mom of this child was about five months pregnant. I asked this mom who had diagnosed this child with diabetes, and she then admitted the child had never really been diagnosed but she had taken her to the doctor before and the doctor told her to watch the child because she could become a diabetic at any time. I asked if there was a family history of diabetes, and she told me that there was none, but she couldn't explain why the doctor had told her the information about the diabetes.

Unknown to this mom, I am a diabetic and very familiar with dietary needs, medications, symptoms, et cetera. When asked about the bruising on the child, the mom explained it as the child always being clumsy and falling. The problem I had with that explanation was that most of the bruising on the child was not in typical areas of where a child would be injured if they fell. Places such as the knees, hands, and elbows. Places that would come in contact with the ground when the child attempted to brace herself from the fall. Things just weren't adding up.

This child had bruises on her ribs, a decubiti sore at the base of her back and on her tail bone to the point that the bone was exposed. Her stomach was distended at the sides, and her buttocks were almost nonexistent. There were bald spots on her head with sores all over her scalp. The distended stomach, sores, and missing hair are all typical signs of malnourishment. The sheriff kept telling me that he didn't believe this to be a case of abuse or neglect because he knew the family and they were good people. Both parents explained the bed sores as being caused by her potty chair. They stated that the child was potty training and loved sitting on the potty chair for long periods of time and that's how she got the decubiti.

While walking through the home, I asked to see the potty chair. The back of the potty chair did not measure up to the location of the decubiti on the child's body, and the potty chair had evidently not been used in a very long time because there was crystallized dried urine in the bottom of the potty itself.

I made it a point to photograph every detail that I was seeing from the Easter baskets to the potty chair. In viewing the child's injuries, I had noticed a bruise on her ribs that looked just like the imprint of an iron. While in the child's bedroom, I observed an iron on the chest of drawers next to the child's bed. The bed also had a large amount of clothes piled on it, and it did not appear to me that the child had been sleeping in her bed.

The mom told me that they had put both children to bed at around nine the night before. She said, at about one thirty in the morning, she woke up to go to the bathroom and looked in on the girls. She said she heard a strange noise coming from the deceased child, so she went in for a closer look, and that's when she discovered the child was not breathing. She said she picked up the child, ran through the living room, into the kitchen area, through a doorway, and into the bathroom with the child. She said she called out for her husband all the while. He was sleeping in the room adjoining the girl's room, according to the mother. She said she ran to the bathroom with the child to splash some cold water on the child to try to help her regain consciousness.

I never understood why she took the long way through the house instead of going through her and her husband's bedroom, which would have been a shorter route to the bathroom and would have allowed her to get her husband's help more quickly. The child had bruising to the head. She explained that by stating she had bumped the child's head on the bathtub as she put the child into the bathtub to splash water on her.

As I checked the child's medical records with the information provided to me by the mother regarding doctors used by the mom, I found that the child had only been taken to the doctor twice in her lifetime—once for a sixth week checkup and once for her sixth month checkup. I could find no other medical records. I tried to interview the sibling, but she could not say a lot at the time, so I placed her in counseling.

Still, at this time, the sheriff or Texas ranger refused to investigate this as a homicide, saying they had to wait until the complete autopsy report was finished. I learned from family members that the mom and dad always distanced them from this child. They would never allow them to have time alone with her. They were always saying that she couldn't go anywhere with them because she was a bad child. The mom referenced many times that people often would ask her what was wrong with the child because she was so small. The mom appeared to enjoy talking about this child's illnesses and being small. I also found out from hospital staff that while the mom was at the emergency room and medical staff was attempting to resuscitate this child, the mother was asking for a sonogram so she could see if she was carrying a boy this time.

Even with all of this, law enforcement was doing nothing about a criminal case. I eventually got permission to remove the oldest child; and when the mom gave birth to her son, I removed him. The final autopsy results were still not in, and it had been months since the child's death, so I called the coroner and explained that I had just removed the newborn child and needed something solid to tell the judge. That is when the coroner confirmed that the child did not die of any natural or medical causes.

When I spoke with our attorney and the attorney ad litem, we contacted the district attorney and asked why nothing was being done regarding charging the parents with the death of this child. We were told that she had never received anything regarding information of this child's death. I was more than happy to provide her with the information that I had gathered as well as the photos that were taken, including the injuries. And before long, the parents were indicted.

As it turned out, when the final autopsy reports came back, the child had died as a result of blunt force trauma to her intestines. The area where there was a rupture was where the bruise that looked like an iron was located. It was also confirmed that the child had been malnourished. There was no sign of diabetes. From everything I gathered in my investigation, it seemed that the mother always liked to be the center of attention. She had the first grandchild, which was the sibling of the deceased child. This birth had gained her some attention, but when she became pregnant with her second child, a sister-in-law was also pregnant. The grandparents had hoped to have a grandson, and the father also had hoped to have a son.

As luck would have it, the mother gave birth to a girl, and the sister-in-law gave birth to a boy. The mother was no longer in the spotlight, so she created imaginary problems with this child by depriving her of food so people would ask about this child being so small. She kept the child distanced from relatives so that they could not see what was really going on. She made up stories about the child being sickly. The father never had much to do with the child.

According to the sibling who eventually started talking, the parents would kick the deceased child, and sometimes she and her sibling would hide under the bed when they heard their father because they were afraid of him. She said most of the punishment her sister would get was because she would try to sneak food from the refrigerator.

To me, it appeared to be a sort of Munchausen case in a way. Nonetheless, this child was a victim of her parents' cruel treatment; the end result was her death. The case was finally tried; the parents were found guilty of murder and sentenced to ninety-nine years. All appeals have been denied, and they continue to serve time in prison. I'm not sure if the sheriff ever believed that the parents murdered this child.

Child death is a very difficult thing to comprehend, especially when it is caused at the hands of the parents of the child. I have never been able to totally comprehend it. Although I was able to explain how and why this child died, I cannot and will not ever be able to understand it fully. The one thing that I learned from this case is that had I not have the support of our legal team, this may have never gotten to trial and these parents may have gotten away with murder. I often drive through the little town where the child lived and stop and gaze at the house where she lived the last minutes of life. The house looks like a house where any normal family would have lived. A swing set in the yard sits empty, and the car the mother drove her children around in still sits in the drive. I wondered if there were ever any happy times for this child. Was she always treated in this manner?

I can still visualize the home as I walked through it, see the Easter baskets with untouched candy and the contents of the fridge; then the pictures of the injuries that I saw on this child would cloud over those memories. What would have appeared to be a normal home to anyone else from the outer appearance turned into a nightmare for that child. I know that God takes care of those little angels and that she is now sheltered in his arms. I like to think that during the time that I was investigating this case that he is the one who guided me to the answers that I found; that through this, this child's voice was finally heard. As I drive away from her home where she lived and died, that is my thought.

Chapter 9

Once my girl was back, it felt good, but it was time for her to start making her own life. She soon moved out and got her own apartment in Sweetwater. By now, I had applied for a job with the state as an investigator of child abuse and had been hired. My daughter decided to go to nursing school, so life seemed to be good again for us. I started working for the state in hopes of having a career of helping children and families in need. Charlie was as supportive as he had always been of the decision I made to change careers. I worked for the state for thirteen years before retiring. During the time that I worked there, I worked on many interesting cases. But the one thing I found out while working there was that things are not always what they seem to be.

While working there, I had some of the poorest excuses for supervisors that a person could have. While not all of my supervisors were that way, most of them were. Another thing I found out was that people did not stay with this job for very long periods of time, and the job itself was not all about taking care of families and children. It seemed to be more about how much grant money could be gotten.

Supervisors who are abusive of their powers should never be a part of a system who takes care of families, especially those who are dishonest. Some, it seemed, would abuse their powers daily as a supervisor, turning staff against each other. It was almost like a game to keep score of who stayed with the job and who didn't. I had a supervisor who lied all of the time. He would make up things just to make me look bad. He would pit other staff against me, and every time he came walking down the hall, I could hear the change jingle in his pockets. I knew that he was coming to my office to make some sort of accusation on me, and I would immediately go into a defense mode.

Sometimes, it would be one or two things that he would make accusations of; sometimes, there would be a whole list of things. It didn't matter to me how many things he accused me of, I knew that I wasn't guilty, and I would not allow him to blame me or admit to the things he accused me of. He accused me of things like taking advantage of other's fourth amendment rights, to talking down to other staff. He once brought in some of my documentation and told me it was sloppy and there were all kinds of misspelled words in the document. When I looked at the document, I saw what he was talking about. But it was definitely not my work. I suspected that he had purposely made some changes sabotaging the work I had done to make it look sloppy and bad.

One of my other coworkers suggested to me that we print off copies of my finished documents before I submitted them to him to see if he was making changes to my work. I started doing this and found out that my suspicions were absolutely correct. He was making the changes after the work was submitted to him. I had begun to come to a point where I avoided him as much as I could because I knew he would come at me with accusations. I had gotten to the point that my blood sugars were raging because of the stress. I wanted so badly to stay with this job because I needed to be able to retire with the benefits. I needed the insurance. My break came when the position for special investigator came open. I had all of the qualifications, so I applied for the job and got it.

After I left his supervision and went to work as a special investigator, I spoke with the program director about his behavior, thinking it would help the staff under him have an easier time. He did apologize to them, but he never apologized to me for what he had done. I believe after being under his supervision, I came away with a sort of PTSD. I had nightmares of the jingling change, and I could hear it in my sleep. I sometimes awakened from my sleep thinking he was in the room to try to reprimand me for something. I hated any kind of authority, and I made it a point of never being wrong on anything.

After the FLDS raid, I worked for a while as a special investigator, but the raid had taken a toll on me. I had spent nearly a year away from my family, and my health seemed to be getting worse. By this time, I was having trouble even getting in and out of my car. Walking was a task in itself, and I felt there was something else going on with my health besides diabetes. I had noticed rashes appearing in different areas of my body during the time I was in the FLDS raids, but I attributed it to being possibly caused by the detergent the hotels were using on the bed sheets. When the rashes didn't stop after I returned home, I started researching the kind of pain I was having and the rashes. I came up with lupus.

I went to my doctor and told her what I believed I had, and she told me that she had watched me walk into her office and she believed that I had rheumatoid arthritis (RA). Once she had run all of the necessary test, we found out that I had both RA and lupus. I was relieved to know that it was something that could be controlled.

By this time, it was noticeable that the investigating staff was quitting their jobs in high numbers. This was creating problems because there were not enough investigators to do the work that needed to be done. Families were not getting the attention they needed, child abuse was a raging thing, and the families were not getting the needed services to help them. This is when the position of peer trainer was created. I applied for this position and was hired to train incoming investigation staff.

If ever I loved a job, it was this one. I had a fantastic supervisor, I loved meeting and training the new staff, and I was able to have hands-on experiences of seeing the cases through while investigators were being trained. I traveled a lot, but that was okay because I was usually home for the most part when night came. The only problem was that this position was short-lived because there were not enough funds to keep the position. I felt it was a big mistake on the state's part for not keeping this position. They should have moved some of the funds around because it seemed that the incoming new investigators were staying with their jobs for longer periods of time and the cases were getting investigated.

I guess everyone loses out when a good program is cut, including the families, because after this, the units went back to not being able to keep staff very long. I eventually became a supervisor for an investigation unit and stayed there until retirement. And I did retire with full benefits. Leaving this job was the best thing I could have done because it was one of the most abusive jobs that I have ever seen. The hours are long, the supervisors are cruel and hateful for the most part, and there is just no gain in the job.

If I could ever give advice to anyone about investigating this entity, I would start with the programs and funding. Find out where the money is being spent and where it needs to be spent. Secondly, weed out those who do not need to be there. Thirdly, don't hire someone who has no life experience. The job itself is about life and how well it should be lived with a family. Fourth, watch those who are supervising because they are the ones who guide and direct the staff. If the staff does not respect them because of their caring attitude, then the staff will not have the caring attitude they should have for this job. There's so much more advice that I could bring to the table after my experiences with this job, but the most important are here.

Some say karma is a real thing, and I believe it. As for the supervisor who jingled his change before coming into my office, he became one of my investigators after being asked to step down or be fired. He couldn't keep up with the pace as he expected his investigators to do, so he resigned. Please don't get me wrong and believe that I didn't like this job—because I had a real heart for it. Even with bad supervision and other obstacles that I had to cross, I had a true heart for these families.

When I left there, I left with a very sour feeling, almost a hatred for the place. About a month after I retired, one of my ex-clients came up to me and congratulated me on my retirement. She said something that made this part of my life worth what I went through. She told me, "You will be deeply missed. Please don't think about the bad things that the job put you through. Know and always remember that you helped at least one family—mine." That left me with a peace of mind that I don't think I would have ever have, had she not told me that.

Today, I see people and children that I worked with; some are adults now. It does me good when they approach me and ask if it's okay to give me a hug. And I hear them say thank you for not giving up on them. This year, I received three invitations to graduations, and last year I received five. Families have sent me pictures of themselves so that I can see that they are doing well and that they are living normal lives as a family together.

So with that said, no amount of jingling change can ever take away from me believing that the job I set out to do was done to the very best it could have been done. And in the end, the petty things like being accused of things I didn't do will one day come out in truth, but I won't be the one who judges. It will be someone with far more knowledge of handling it than me. I look forward to that day.

Kerrie at her college graduation pictured with her granddaughter

CPS sleeve patch worn by Kerrie Bullard

Chapter 10

Losing a spouse is never easy, no matter how young or how old you are. Charlie had been having Transient Ischemic Attack (small strokes) and had fallen several times. At first, we weren't sure what was going on until he saw a neurologist. The neurologist told Charlie that as a result of his uncontrolled diabetes and being overweight, he would have to lose up to fifty pounds, get on a strict diet, and have some rehabilitative stuff, or he would not survive this.

Charlie had always been a very strong man, but he seemed so weak at this time. It was a scary time for both of us. I had never seen him like this. Charlie had always been my rock and my strength. I just knew that we had to deal with this so that he could be strong again. I don't really think that I faced the whole truth honestly. I believe that in a childlike way, I thought everything would just go back to the way it had been as soon as we did everything the doctor said we should.

Charlie was a little unwilling to help himself at first. By now, we had gotten him on disability because he was unable to work with the falls and everything else that was going on. I worried on a daily basis because we lived in the country; I left for work early and sometimes did not return until after dark. Sometimes, when Charlie would fall, we would struggle to get him out of the floor for anywhere from fifteen minutes or longer. Luckily, most of the times he fell, I was there to help him up; and on one time, the meter reader came in to help because I couldn't get him up. My worry was that he would fall and I wouldn't be there to help him. When he fell, he was deadweight and couldn't get up by himself.

I didn't know what I was going to do to get him to let me help him, so I went to a co-worker at Adult Protective Services and asked for advice. Her advice was simply to call an intake in and report Charlie's self- abuse and unwillingness to help himself. It was a hard call to make, but making that call was going to get him the help he needed, so I made the call and report.

I can remember the day I sat down and had a long talk with Charlie. When I got home, I told Charlie that we needed to discuss things. I explained to him about me calling Adult Protective Services and why I had called. This was the first time in months that Charlie and I had really openly communicated. It was like being in the room with the old Charlie. We talked about a lot of things. We talked for over two hours.

I asked Charlie a question that I had to know the answer to. I asked him that if anything happened and he passed away before me, if he would be in heaven waiting for me when I get there. He told me that beyond a shadow of a doubt, he knew that he would be there waiting for me and that he knew that Christ was in his heart. We both cried as we spoke about this. It was a relief for me to know that he would not spend an eternity in hell if he went before me. I don't think this conversation would have been an easy one if Charlie had not told me that he is a Christian.

The investigator from Adult Protective Services contacted Charlie and put some things in motion for Charlie to not only get with a dietician but to get rehab. She made arrangements for him to go into the nursing home for six weeks for this. We were both saddened but happy at the same time. We talked about it, and I stressed to Charlie that a lot of people believe the nursing home is a final place to go before dying. But in his case, this would be the place he would be going to start living again. He agreed and seemed kind of relieved that help was on the way.

Sundays were always a very busy day for me because I went to church in Sweetwater and we lived in Rotan. I played piano for the church, so I would stay at my parents' house on Sunday. It was a Sunday on the day before Charlie was to go into the nursing home for rehab. I went to church as usual, and Charlie and I talked by phone that afternoon like we always did. We spent about an hour on the phone. He was washing all of his clothing and getting ready to go.

I had been shopping for a television set for him and bought some of the toiletries he needed. I went to church for the evening services. As I started to leave the parking lot, I looked at my cell phone and noticed there were three missed calls from our house. There were two messages.

As I listened, I could hear the agony in Charlie's voice as he told me that he was having some stomach problems like he had never had before and he was going to call for an ambulance.

I immediately tried to call home but got no answer, so I called the Fisher County Sheriff Department and asked if the ambulance was at my house. They confirmed that they were there and said I should meet them at the Fisher County Hospital; the paramedics reported that I should get there quickly. I called my mom who had just gotten home from church and informed her of what was going on. She told me that she and Dad would get there as quickly as they could. I don't remember much about the drive to the hospital. I think I was in shock. I had just spoken to Charlie a few hours earlier, and he was doing well. I didn't know what to expect when I got there.

I actually arrived at the hospital before Charlie did. As I waited for the ambulance to arrive, the doctor met with me and told me things appeared to be pretty serious. He said that from what the paramedics had relayed to him, Charlie either had an abdominal aneurysm or a tear in his colon. He told me when Charlie arrived that he would do a series of x-rays to determine, but in either event, the Fisher County Hospital would not be able to handle this and Charlie would be airflighted to Lubbock.

When Charlie arrived, he was in a great deal of pain, and it was obvious. As the doctor worked to find out what was going on, my mom and dad came, followed by my daughter and daughter-in-law. As I sat with Charlie in the emergency room, he told me that he had never been in so much pain. He said that he was afraid. I prayed with him in the silence of him and I being in the room alone for a few minutes. I prayed that God would just lay his hand on Charlie and take away the fear and pain. I was glad that we had those few minutes alone because after that, everything moved pretty fast.

The doctor came in and confirmed that the x-ray had displayed a tear in Charlie's intestine and that he would need to be flown immediately to Lubbock for surgery to repair it. My son lived in Lubbock at the time, so I made arrangements for him to be there waiting for Charlie when he arrived at the hospital. My mom went with me to Lubbock in the car. When I arrived there, for some reason I thought the hospital would already have Charlie in surgery; instead, he was still in the emergency room, and my son was sitting in there with him. My son told me that only a nurse had been in there, so I went to the nurse's station and asked where the doctor was.

I was told that a doctor would come as soon as one was available and not until. I told them that Charlie was in pain and that the doctor in Rotan had said it was an emergency to get Charlie to Lubbock so that the tear in his intestine could be repaired. The nurse assured me that there was no tear in Charlie's intestine and that he did not need surgery. But with that, he couldn't explain the pain Charlie was having and said they were going to control it with medication and watch him a while.

We stayed in the emergency room until about 5:00 a.m., and at that time, medical staff came in and said they had a room for Charlie and were going to move him there for observation. My mom and I were allowed to stay in the room with him. By now, he was sleeping pretty soundly as the morphine had kicked in pretty good. I stayed in a recliner next to his bed, and Mom stayed in a cot at the foot of his bed.

At around seven thirty, my daughter, who is a nurse, had arrived. She noticed what appeared to be stones in his catheter bag. We showed it to medical staff who in turn called in a doctor. Charlie was awake again by this time, kind of drifting in and out. The doctor came in and began yelling at me about bringing him to their hospital. I tried to explain that he had been airlifted there, and she told me that he was probably going to die. She said she had tried to talk to me about this before, but I was not in his room when she came. I had not left Charlie's side nor had my mother.

Charlie heard everything this doctor said, and he motioned for me to come to his side. He said to me that he did not believe he was going to make it through this alive. I told him not to listen to what the doctor had said because the one who was in control was not this doctor, it was God. I then went into the hallway, spoke with the doctor about her bedside manners, and very quickly told her not to come near Charlie again. She attempted to deny the way she had spoken, but I stood my ground and discharged her. I then went to the nursing station and asked for another doctor.

By this time, plans were being made to get Charlie into surgery because the medical staff believed that he had kidney stones and said they were going to put some stints in him. I was told the whole procedure would take about forty-five minutes. As they took him into surgery, Charlie told me that if something happened and he didn't make it through this, he wanted to be cremated. He and I had talked about this before, but I didn't believe this would be a reality. I kissed Charlie and told him how much I loved him and what he had meant to me in my life. He had been everything to me—a father to my children, my husband, my friend, my love, and my life . . . I couldn't imagine going through the rest of my life without him. I smiled at him, and we told each other again that we loved each other. That is the last thing Charlie said to me before going off down the hall with the surgical team.

My daughter, mother, son, and I were escorted to a waiting room where we were told that a doctor would come and talk to us after the surgery. As we sat in the waiting room, talking nervously about little things that really didn't matter, I began to notice that the time was passing the marker of forty-five minutes and soon it would have been an hour and a half. I began to believe something was wrong, so I went to the nurse's station. I could tell by the look on the nurses' faces that something was wrong. I can remember the nurse saying to me, "Oh, Ms. Blair, the doctor hasn't told you?" When I asked what the doctor had not told me, I saw them bringing Charlie around the corner. He was connected to a life support system.

I stood there in shock. I remember the nurse saying, "Don't worry, he will probably be okay. He went into cardiac arrest in surgery. Just give it some time." When I think back on it, I have often wondered why a doctor didn't come out and tell me what had happened. Not one time did I ever talk to that doctor, so I will never for sure know why Charlie went into cardiac arrest. I was in shock, in disbelief. From there, things kind of moved in slow motion. They took Charlie to ICU and escorted me and my mom to a family waiting room. By now, it was the middle of the night. The nurse said there were blankets and pillows in there and we could use the lounge sofas to sleep, so that if there was a change, she would be able to notify us quickly.

My mom and I both tried to sleep, but it was just so difficult. This was like a bad dream that I could not wake up from. I kept thinking that Charlie would wake up and life could just go back to normal. About three hours after he was taken to ICU, the nurse came and got me. She told me that Charlie was trying to wake up. I went to him, but he did not act like he recognized me. He had a strange look in his eyes like he really wasn't there. I sat and talked with him and told him that I would be there when he was ready to totally wake up, to keep getting better and stronger. I prayed for him while I was in there with him. I prayed that God would just give me some sign that it would be okay.

When I went back into the family waiting room, dawn was just beginning. The families in the waiting room were starting to wake up. As I sat with my mom, I looked across the room. I could not believe my eyes. There were two ladies there that I recognized. They were now women, but I had known them in my childhood; they had attended Sunday school with me. Their eyes caught mine about the same time, and it was evident that they recognized me. For the first time in two days, something seemed normal and familiar. I showed my mom, and we headed toward each other. Their mom was in ICU and not doing well. They were so helpful. They gave me a brochure about a place to stay just two blocks down the street. It was definitely a Godsend to have them there, for nothing had been normal since I had picked up my phone and listened to the messages left by Charlie.

We talked and cried together about what this experience had been like for us. Oh, how I longed to just get Charlie and take him home with me so that we could go back to our life at our house in the country in Fisher County, but this was not going to happen any time soon. Unfortunately, my friend's mom passed away during our time there. I can remember late one night seeing a young girl and her mother being brought into the family waiting room just as my mom and I had been a few days before. They had the same lost look that my mom and I must have had when we entered that room. I made my way over to them and introduced myself to them. I knew what a lost feeling it was to come into that room—the unknown. I showed them around and helped them find a pillow and blanket, and I gave them the same brochure that my childhood friend had given to me. The girl's father had a stroke and had been airlifted from Farmington, New Mexico. He also was on life support. We became very good friends over the next few days.

By now, Charlie's daughter had arrived and was staying there with me to give my mom some relief so that she could go home and care for my father. Every day, I would get to the hospital at 5:00 a.m., hoping to talk to a doctor; every day, I would be disappointed. I would stay as late as they would let me and spend as much time as I could with Charlie. His daughter and I took turns. She was always so good to give Charlie and me time to ourselves. I would talk to him and hope that he was hearing every word that I would say. I talked about his grandchildren, things they were doing, about people who had been to see him, and about how much I missed him.

Sometimes, he would squeeze my hand on command. But the neurologist finally told me that this was a normal infantile reaction, that an infant automatically squeezes your hand when you put your finger out. He said that we are born with that instinct, and this did not necessarily mean that Charlie was hearing or improving. In fact, he told me that I was going to need to think about making some decisions. He said if there was no improvement within two weeks, I could either disconnect the life support system or have Charlie moved to a nursing home with the life support.

When Charlie and I had talked at home on many occasions, one of the things that we made very clear to each other was that neither of us wanted to be kept alive on life support. We both had agreed that if it came to that, to disconnect. I prayed so hard about it. I did not want to make the decision to disconnect him from his life support.

The twenty-ninth of March marked our twenty-third anniversary. I spent the evening with Charlie. I sang to him the song "You're My Only Love." I asked him not to leave me on our anniversary. I kissed him before leaving and told him how much our life together had meant and how truly blessed my children and I were for having him in our lives. I held his hand as I spoke with him, and I really believe that he heard every word I spoke to him because he didn't leave me that night.

Two days before my final decision had to be made, I heard a page for the anesthesiologist to come to ICU. Just before the page, a man had sat down in the chair beside me. He began talking to me in a very kind and soft voice. I had never seen this man before, but he was talking to me as if he had known me forever. Why I sat and listened, I can't say, but he was very calming and reassuring. He told me that no matter what pain I was going through with my loved one, God knew everything that I had endured through this and that Charlie was in a good place in his life. It didn't dawn on me that he had called Charlie by his name or how he knew Charlie's name until later when I was rethinking everything.

While this man was speaking to me, a lady came into the waiting room and called for me. As I walked up to her, I knew that the time had come for a decision. I could tell by the look on her face. She told me that a nurse was cleaning the tubing around Charlie's esophageal airway and had broken the tubing. She said they could not get the airway back in; they were either going to have to do a tracheotomy or take him off. I looked at his daughter and asked her what she wanted to do. She said that she knew that her dad didn't want to be on life support, so we made the decision not to put him back on it.

I asked to see Charlie, and they took me in to his room. As I left the area where I had been listening to this strange man, I noticed that he was no longer sitting in the chair. I searched the room but didn't see him anywhere. When I got to his room, Charlie's eyes were open. He looked as if he was absolutely terrified. I began talking to him and stroking his hand. I told him that I loved him and knew what his wishes were. I told him that I would not let anyone hurt him, that it was okay to let go or stay, and that the choice was now his. He calmed down as I spoke to him, and for just a minute, it looked like he may have recognized me for the first time in days. The soft look that I had grown to love so much in Charlie came back to his eyes for just a second as I held his hand and wiped his face with a cool cloth. Then he closed his eyes, but the look on his face was a peaceful look.

I left long enough to call my mom and the rest of the family to let them know what was going on, and I gathered my composure and went back into his room. I didn't leave for the next fourteen hours. As Charlie struggled with life, I sat next to his bed stroking his hand and talking to him to let him know that I was there with him and his daughter was there also. By now, my mom, daughter, and son had gotten there also. Early in the morning, Charlie began to breathe easier, and he very peacefully went on April 3. He didn't leave me on our anniversary.

It is definitely not like they show it to be on television. You know the scene where they unplug the machines and disconnect everything, and in just a few seconds the heart stops, you hear that beep turning into one long tone, and then everyone leaves the room. It didn't happen that way at all. Charlie lingered for fourteen hours, but for the most part, it was a peaceful fourteen hours with him. I know that I will see Charlie again in heaven. I know that he is better off where he is. But sometimes, for just a minute, I catch a glimpse of someone who reminds me of him. I catch myself looking closely at them for little details that I knew about him such as a scar, a dimple, or even the light in the eyes that I loved in Charlie so much. Then I realize that my Charlie is in heaven waiting for me to get there.

The man in the waiting room was never seen again, and when I mentioned it to Charlie's daughter, she told me that she never saw anyone sitting beside me. I believe that God can make contact with you in many ways, and I believe that day God walked into the room with me for long enough to let me know that it was okay to let go of what I had been holding on to so desperately—my Charlie. As for the cause of all of this, after the autopsy was completed, it was discovered that seventeen centimeters of Charlie's colon was ruptured, and gangrene had set in. So the doctor in the little town of Rotan was right, and the doctors in the big city of Lubbock, Texas, were wrong.

The time after Charlie's death when everyone went home and my house was quiet was the hardest. I would catch myself rethinking everything over and over again, questioning myself for the decisions that I made. I couldn't sleep at night. It was too dark and too quiet. I found myself leaving lights on throughout the house and televisions playing to make some noise. One day, I woke up thinking to myself that I had to get some normal back into my life. I began to think about things I loved about Charlie and what I had learned from those things. I began to keep a journal. I wrote things down that I would tell Charlie if he were there with me. This helped me with the healing process.

I think it was Charlie's way of reaching out to me one last time to let me know that it was okay to go on with my life and live. I learned from Charlie that life is good and heaven is for real, to laugh often and enjoy life. I learned that sometimes the quiet times are good to have to process life in itself. I learned that God does hear prayers and that he answers them in his time. But most of all, I learned that it is okay to live after you lose, and that losing is not the end.

Charlie and Kerrie at wedding reception

Chapter 11

After Charlie died, I do not remember a lot about the following year. Some people say that God just gives your body a break by allowing you to function but not remember things that cause pain. I think that's true in my case. I can remember that the one thing I wanted most after Charlie died was to have something normal back in my life. Nothing seemed normal. The house was always quiet, there was no one to prepare meals for, and I didn't hear Charlie's snoring at night.

I had moved to Sweetwater from the house Charlie and I had owned in Rotan. I do not even remember moving. I remember my brother-in-law showing me the house in Sweetwater and saying that I should buy it, but after that, there is not much that I remember. I did buy that house, and I have a vague memory of signing papers for this house. I know that there were people who helped me move, but I have very little memory of that. I don't really know when I moved into the house in Sweetwater. It's like one day I woke up and I was there.

I do remember that the guy came to connect the satellite and my granddaughters were with me. My youngest granddaughter loved to brush my waist-length hair. She was standing behind me on the sofa, and I was talking to the installation guy when I felt this tugging on my hair. I asked my granddaughter what she was doing. To make a long story short, she had wrapped my hair around the brush, and it was so tangled into the brush that it would not come loose. I really thought I had no choice but to cut off my waist-length hair. The satellite installation guy was very young but so sweet. He urged me not to get my hair cut and to let him untangle the mess my granddaughter had made in my hair. He very carefully worked at getting the brush loose from my hair for about forty-five minutes. I was so grateful that this young man had taken the time to do this.

As it turned out, he was eighteen years old, working his very first job, and turned out to be the grandson of one of the people I went to church with. I have never forgotten him and the time that he gave to get my hair untangled from the brush. To some, this may not seem like much, but to me it meant a lot. It was one of the few things that I do remember. At night, I didn't sleep well. It was so quiet. I was used to hearing Charlie snore. I never thought that I would miss that sound, but I did. Sometimes, it was so quiet that I would turn on all of the televisions just to have some noise. I would leave lights on throughout the house because it was so dark, and I didn't like the dark.

The only thing normal in my life right now was going to work. That was a constant; it never changed. I saw the same people every day that I had seen and worked with for years. It seemed that the people that I had investigated in the past kept coming back around for more investigations, so that was also normal. At least I had this to help me through this time. Even when I went to church, it seemed like things were different. The services were the same, and the people were the same, but it seemed different. The sweet spirit that I had once felt in that placed seemed to have diminished. I didn't feel the presence of God like I once had, and I felt so very alone. Maybe it was because that's where I was when I received the call from Charlie telling me how sick he was. I just don't know, but it was not the same anymore.

I remember thinking to myself that life should not be like this, but I was grasping at everything that I could to make my life normal again. I couldn't really explain my feelings to my mom or dad because I didn't understand them myself. It was something that I had never been through. My daughter and her husband were busy with their life, and my son was in Lubbock, Texas, working. My grandchildren would come on the weekends, and my ex-daughter-in-law would try to fit me into her life, but she was working all of the time. My sweet mom and dad tried their best to make things simple for me by fixing dinner for me every night, but this was not the answer, and it was not their responsibility to make my life normal.

One Friday evening, I called a friend who was also a widow and asked her if she wanted to go out for the evening. She said that she would like to get out. Earlier in the week, I had heard about this thing called karaoke, so we decided we would go to this karaoke place. After all, I loved singing and felt like it would be fun. I was a little uncomfortable because the karaoke was in a bar, but I was ready to do something to make a change in this place in my life that I seemed to be stuck in. I was searching for something that would help me have something that I knew back into my life. I was so totally lost.

We walked into the bar where it was. I had not been inside a bar for at least eighteen years, but the atmosphere was all so familiar to me. For the first time since I had received that phone call that Charlie was being taken to the hospital, I felt like I was exactly where I belonged. People were very friendly, and everyone was happy and having a good time. I didn't really know many people in there, but I felt like I did. I knew it was wrong to be here in this place, but for the few hours I was there, there wasn't any silence or darkness in my life. There was laughter, music, and it seemed right.

I didn't know it when we first went into the bar, but later I found out I knew the owner casually, and she made me feel at home there. She asked me and my friend to sit at her table with her, and she got me up to do karaoke very quickly. I loved this feeling. For the first time in almost a year, I felt like the part of me that had been missing was back. I felt alive, and I felt like I belonged here. As my friend and I sat at that table, a gentleman came over to me and asked if he could buy me a drink. I told him that I was drinking diet Coke and didn't drink alcohol. He told me that I could have as many diet Cokes as I wanted and they were all on him.

This man also told me that he had admired me from a distance for many years and that he had asked about me before and found out that I was married. He then told me that he had heard about the loss of Charlie and that he was very sorry to hear about Charlie's death. That felt kind of eerie; almost like this man had been stalking me. Eventually, the man asked me to dance with him. I was reluctant because it had been so long since I had danced, but I soon found out that it came back to me very quickly. As we danced, this man told me that he was a local business owner, divorced for eight years, and had never had any children. He told me that he wanted to have a minute of my time because he didn't want the night to get away without me knowing who he was.

As I sat at the table, this man sat down and continued talking to me throughout the night. As the night was ending, he asked me if I would be back for karaoke the next week, and I didn't really give him an answer. He told me that he would be there and he would look for me. I really did not know how to take this. It had been over twenty-three years since a man had pursued me in that manner, and I felt clumsy at it. Almost embarrassed! Charlie had now been gone for eight months. I wasn't sure if the timing was right for me to even be thinking about seeing another man. I would just have to let God take this one and do whatever he felt was best for me. I knew that going to a bar was not the right thing for me to be doing, but it kept me from feeling so out of place. I was familiar with that atmosphere because of when Charlie and I had played in bands. I was familiar with performing in front of people because of when Charlie and I had played in bands. I guess I was just looking for anything that would take me back to Charlie, and this did.

The next week, for some reason, the admin technician from our sister office in Snyder, Texas, called me and asked if I knew anyone who built tents. I told her about the man I had met on the weekend. He had told me that he owned a business and that it was a canvas business. I gave her the information and forgot about it until about a week later when she called back and asked me to call and see if the tent was ready. I asked her to call him herself, and she said the welfare board really needed the tent; if I called, he might hurry with the order since he knew me.

When I called the canvas business, a lady answered the phone. I told her who I was, who I worked for, and what I needed. I asked her about the tent, and she told me that her boss needed to talk to me. I tried to stop her from getting him on the phone, but it was too late; she had put me on hold. When he came on the phone, he asked me if I worked in Snyder, Texas, too. I told him that Snyder was one of the many areas I worked. He told me that he would come personally and set up the tent if I would be there, so I agreed.

When he and his crew showed up to put up the tent, I was there as I had promised. To me, it was a little awkward, but he treated it very casually and was very nice. After the tent was set up, I was leaving to go back to Sweetwater when he told me that he had dismissed his crew and that he needed a ride home. I really did not know how to take this, but I felt like I may as well not fight it since he had been nice enough to bring the tent and set it up at no charge, so I told him I would give him a ride.

On the trip home, he grabbed my hand very carefully and began to stroke my arm. I was so nervous that I drove off the road, and then I was embarrassed. I wasn't sure if this was what I wanted or not, but regardless, it was here. Should I jerk my hand back and slap him, or should I just sit there like a bump on a log? It almost felt right. It felt normal. It felt like I belonged again. All of the sad feelings I had been feeling seemed to be diminishing, and I was beginning to feel happy again.

This is when I met Jerry, my husband now. Time moved on through our relationship, and we began to know each other very well. He made me feel comfortable about our relationship. He made me feel like I belonged there. For the first time since the whole ordeal with Charlie had begun, I was beginning to feel like I was having some normal back in my life again. I remember the night that Jerry proposed to me. He told me that I was at home with him. He told me that he loved me and would make me happy for the rest of our life. That was nearly eleven years ago.

Through the first year, we made many changes. Although I felt familiar with the bar scene, it was not right, and I knew it. I stopped going there, and Jerry stopped drinking alcohol. He also stopped smoking. He also stopped going to the bar. I started going back to church again. This was my other home. I had left it for a short time, but I knew that God was still my God. I knew that God had put all of these circumstances in front of me for a reason, that he brought people into my life for reasons, and that Jerry was one of them. I also believe that he brought me into Jerry's life for a reason. Jerry became very ill not long after we married. He began bleeding internally. Because of my past medical training, I recognized the symptoms. I took him immediately to the hospital for treatment.

After surgery, he recovered. He will always deal with the repercussions of drinking alcohol for so long, but he is happy, alive, and no longer drinking alcohol. Time has been good for us through the years, and I am glad that God did put Jerry in my life. I have retired from my job with the state, and I now work alongside with Jerry at the canvas business. There is much less stress in my life, which is good. I think if Charlie could tell me something now, it would be that he wants me to live life and be happy, to feel at home, and enjoy everything around me. I believe that he would tell me to make the right choices for myself and keep God very close in sight when doing so. I believe if he could have chosen someone for me, he would have chosen Jerry. I know this for certain—I am now at home.

I still have a hard time thinking clearly when it comes to what happened with Charlie. When people begin to talk to me about that time, I have a tendency to have some loss of memory. I am not for sure if it is because I don't want to remember or if it is because I am being protected from those memories. For a while, those times of wanting normal back in my life would come and go. But now it's no longer an issue because I am at home with Jerry, and my life is like it should be. As for the life in the bars, I have asked for God's forgiveness for letting him down in that aspect. I know that he has forgiven me because he is a forgiving God always, and his arms are always opened wide for his children. I am a child of God. I asked him to give me another opportunity to serve him again, and he sent me a church that was in need of an organist.

I now serve him faithfully, and I thank him every day for this opportunity. It is an honor and a privilege that I will never under estimate. I love the song "His Eye is on the Sparrow," and I know he watches me. It has very special meaning to me because I know that through the last hours of my grandfather, dad, and Charlie's life, God was watching over us all. I could feel his perfect peace, and I saw it on their faces as they left this world.

There was one time in the bar when, at closing time, I went into the restroom to wash my hands. I found a church track that had been left there by someone. As I read it, I knew that this was God's way of telling me that these feelings of being at home in the bar were just a false pretense sent to me by Satan, something that was put there before me to mask those feelings of loss that I had been feeling. I didn't put my trust in God to get me through those rough times after the loss of Charlie, and the further I got away from God, the closer Satan got to me. I will always believe that God put Jerry in my life and me in Jerry's life. We both needed someone to guide us away from that life and back into the life that God intended for us to live. God is good all of the time, every day, every second, minute, and every hour. God is in control, and his timing is perfect.

Mother's Day 2014 with Kerrie Bullard, her
mom, and her two granddaughters

Jerry and Kerrie Bullard

Chapter 12

I knew something was not totally right with my daughter. She was now married, an adult, and seeming to have more needs than she ever had. With the death of Charlie behind us for nearly a year, I started noticing that my daughter and her husband were having more and more trouble paying their bills. She would often call and ask for a loan until her next paycheck. She would blame it on her husband's race car business. She said he was spending more money than they had on his car.

I often explained to her that they needed to set a budget for the racing business and a budget for their household needs. She would agree, but then a week or two later, she would call asking for a loan. At first, it seemed to bother her to ask me for the loans, but after a while, it seemed to just come out naturally. I had just met Jerry and was in the beginning stages of a relationship with him. I was extremely angered when he once told me that he believed that my daughter and her husband may be using drugs and he felt they were taking advantage of me. He told me that he didn't want me to be the one who was hurt in the end. We didn't exactly argue about this, but I did in no uncertain terms tell this man that it was none of his business and he should stay out of it.

I had never known my daughter to be dependent on any type of drugs or alcohol. I started paying more attention to details, like when I would drive out to their house, they always met me at the car. I hardly ever was invited into their home. My daughter's husband would disappear very quickly, and there were always people that I didn't know at their house. I began questioning myself if I was possibly helping them have a drug habit by enabling them through loaning. Being the parent of someone who is possibly using drugs is not an easy thing. As the parent of a child you have raised and loved, it is hard to see the imperfections they have, and admitting to it is even harder.

The relationship with Jerry grew stronger, and I had started becoming very ill. I had type one diabetes for a very long time, so I was used to dealing with that, but this was different. I had started having some really intense back pain. One night, the pain was so bad that I had to call a friend to take me to the emergency room. I tried to call my daughter, but she didn't answer her phone. In the emergency room, it was determined that I had a very bad kidney infection and that my blood sugars were soaring nearly to five hundred. I was so out of it; I didn't question the doctor when he gave me an antibiotic and a pain shot and sent me home. I was on an insulin pump, and there is no way that my sugars should have ever gotten that high with the pump.

Once at home, my friend offered to stay with me. But being out of it like I was, I told her not to stay, so she left. The next morning, Jerry came by and saw that I was sick. He had his own business and had to go out of town. He offered to stay, but I told him to go on, so he did. Even though he was a type two diabetic, he didn't fully understand the seriousness of what was going on. I don't remember much after that, except at some point I woke up and my friend who had taken me to the ER during the night was standing at the end of my bed, calling out to me. I don't even know how she got into my house. She told me that I didn't look very good, and she wanted to take me back to the ER. I told her to just let me rest, and I would probably feel better later. I don't remember her leaving.

The next thing I remember was an alarm sounding from my insulin pump. I was very familiar with this pump and the way it worked because I had worn it for ten years, but for some reason I couldn't get it together and stop the alarm. I called my daughter again, and this time, she answered. She said she would come and help me, but it seemed like she really didn't want to. I somehow managed to call my endocrinologist in Lubbock, Texas, and he told me that he wanted me to come straight to the ER in Lubbock. He attempted to get me to let him call an ambulance, but I was so out of it. I told him that my daughter was bringing me.

I don't know how long it was before my daughter finally arrived at my house because I fell back asleep, but she came and told me that we would have to take my car because she didn't have enough gas and her husband needed her car, so we started out for Lubbock. As we pulled out of the drive, she told me she had made candles for someone and needed to take them to that person before we left town. She also had some crayons that belonged to some kid of a friend, so she needed to make that stop too. Then she said she had to go by her house and feed her dog. Finally, we were on the two-hour trip to Lubbock. She wanted to stop at a convenience store to smoke because I didn't allow smoking in my car. I believe it was then that she realized how truly ill I was. I remember her starting to cry and telling me that she didn't realize how sick I was. I told her to just get me to Lubbock where I could find out what was going on.

When we finally arrived in Lubbock, I remember my doctor asking what took so long to get there and my daughter making up excuses. When he checked my blood sugars, they had soared up to 1,400. I was admitted into ICU. I really don't remember much except as they took me in I recognized the nurse in ICU. She recognized me as it had not been that long ago that I had sat with Charlie in that very ICU as he lived his last hours on earth. My son arrived at the hospital. He lived in Lubbock. I don't even remember if I spoke to him; I was so out of it.

They started to put me in the same room that Charlie had been in, but the nurse that recognized me stopped them and explained that my husband had passed away in that room. The doctor came in and told me that I had nephritis. I had no idea what this was but was relieved that something was going to be done. After that, I don't remember much except that I woke up and this strange woman that I didn't know was standing beside my bed. She told me that she was Jerry's sister. She said someone had (and I don't know who) had called him and told him I had been taken to Lubbock. He had called her and asked her to let me know that he was on his way here.

One of the businesses he owned was in Lubbock, so he could work from there too. He showed up and stayed with me there in Lubbock the whole time I was there. I was in ICU for seventeen days and then put on the medical floor until I could be released. My mom was in Abilene in the hospital at the time because she had knee surgery, and I had been so out of it that I had not let her know where I was. Jerry went to Abilene and told her where I was and what had happened. My dad was very ill and required care, so my daughter reluctantly agreed to check on him daily.

During the time that I was so ill, my daughter never came to the hospital to see me, which was so unlike her. We had always been so close. After the death of Charlie, my daughter lost her paternal grandfather. She was very close to him. It also took a grave toll on her. She had a hard time accepting Charlie's death, the death of her grandfather, and now me seeing another man. She really didn't like that at all. As time went from summer to winter, I became sicker. It seemed like every other week I was in the Lubbock Hospital ICU with high blood sugars and kidney problems. Finally, after a lot of research and testing, my doctor discovered a rather large kidney stone blocking infection up into my left kidney to the point that my left kidney had quit functioning. Eventually, my left kidney was removed to prevent further damage of the right kidney.

By now I was going to be married to Jerry. On the day of our wedding, things with my daughter was just not right. She showed up at my wedding without her husband, and he showed up later. Neither of them was much dressed for the occasion. I noticed they sat in different places at the wedding. I took a minute to talk with her, and she told me they were separating. But at the reception, she showed me some scratches on her hand where she told me that her husband had held her down and tried to shove a sock in her mouth. She said they were fighting but wouldn't tell me what they were fighting about. He was not at the reception, so I was unable to talk to him.

After the wedding and after things settled down, I spoke with her husband. He admitted to me that he and my daughter had been using methamphetamines. He told me that he had given it to her in the beginning, but she had really become addicted to the drug. I confronted her, and she admitted to using the drug but said she had stopped. I knew that this is not a drug that a person could just quit using. One day, she called me and said her pain level in her stomach was so bad that she thought she had appendicitis. I immediately took her to the ER. I don't think we were prepared for what we found out. My daughter had always wanted a child but had never been able to conceive one. At this time, we found that she was having an atopic pregnancy, and the baby would have to be aborted. This absolutely crushed her spirit.

Although there is no real excuse for drug use, I will always believe that losing Charlie as we did, her grandfather dying so suddenly after Charlie's death, the loss of her marriage, and the loss of the baby attributed to her addiction. I lived in constant fear that one day I would receive a phone call either telling me that she was dead or that she had been arrested. It was evident that she was hanging around people who were dangerous and very involved in some illegal activity. I was approached by people on our task force who told me they were watching her and that she was involved very deeply with drug trafficking and weapons trafficking.

I begged her to stop, but this girl who I had known as my beautiful daughter was no longer the girl that I had raised. She was almost like a monster out of control. I did not like who she had become. If she was high, she was happy; if she was coming down off of the drugs, she was hateful and mean. She would do anything to get her meth.

Charlie and I shared a time of playing music together in our younger days. Charlie played bass guitar. After he died, I placed those guitars in a closet where they would be safe. One day, I opened the closet and noticed one of the guitars was missing. My heart sank as low as it could get because I knew that she had taken it to a pawnshop. She denied it. I called a detective that I knew in the Pawn Shop Detail, and he immediately found the guitar with her name on the pawn ticket. He told me to tell her that she could either go and pick it up from the pawnshop herself, or he would take it as evidence and press charges on her for stealing it.

After everything that I found out, she still continued to deny that she took it, even when she brought it back to me. That is one of the evils of drugs. They take the person you love and turn them into someone you don't know, someone you would never dream that you would ever associate with.

Then it finally happened. My phone rang on Thanksgiving morning at about one-thirty in 2005. My heart raced as I answered the phone. It is usually not good news when you get a call at that time of the morning. The voice on the other end introduced himself as a police officer from Taylor County. I don't remember his name, but I remember the rest of the sentence when he told me that my daughter had been arrested with eight grams of meth in her possession. I breathed a sigh of relief. She was still alive. He wanted to know if I would come and get her and post her bond. I had to tell him that she could wait until morning, and if I came, she needed to have the money to make her bond. She told him that she did, and I agreed to go and get her the next morning.

Growing up in Fisher County with a mom as a cop, my daughter had learned several things—she could get by with just about anything by flaunting my name and that she usually didn't have to pay the price for getting into trouble because the judge in Fisher County liked her so much and thought of her as a granddaughter rather than a citizen of Fisher County who had done something wrong. And even though I had discouraged it, the one time that my daughter got caught with beer and driving without a license, the judge dismissed the charges.

I had two reasons for waiting until morning to pick my daughter up. First, I did not want to be on the highway that time of the morning alone on a holiday, and second, I wanted her to know what it was like to be locked up; to actually hear the doors closing behind her and feel the confinement of being locked up.

I barely slept the rest of the night, but at least I did have the peace of mind that she was somewhere where she would be safe. I arrived at the Taylor County jail about eleven that morning. Our Thanksgiving had already been ruined, so I didn't have to worry about cooking for the first time in years, nor did I have guests that year. As I walked into the jail, I had to ring some sort of a phone system that called back to the jail, and then they told me to sit down at a glass window and wait for my daughter to appear on the other side.

Although I had been around jails as a cop for most of my adult life, I had a very uneasy feeling while I was there, and I could not wait until I got out of there either. My daughter finally appeared. She looked tired, and she was wearing jail attire. This was one of the hardest things for me to see even though I knew it was probably the best thing she could ever experience. I remember when I taught the DARE program in the Fisher County Schools, I would give the students a tour through the jail. I would ask who wanted to go into a cell. And for those who volunteered, I would close the cell door and lock it, leaving the students in the cell for about five minutes. After I opened the door, I had each of them talk individually about how it made them feel to be enclosed in the cell and not be able to leave when they were ready.

For the most part, I would hear comments like "Although I knew that you wouldn't leave me here, and I would get out in a few minutes,

I felt like I had totally lost control of my life. When you opened the door, I felt a total feeling of relief." As I talked to my daughter through the glass on the phone, she begged me to hurry and get her out of there. Oh, how I wanted to hold her on my lap as I did while she was just a little girl and sing to her "You Are My Sunshine." Even though she was an adult, she seemed almost childlike again because she was dependent on me to get her out. As luck would have it, I ran into a bondsman there that I had known from previous years as a cop. He asked why I was there, and I told him about my daughter being arrested. I believe this was the first step of God intervening because he is the one who bonded out my daughter at a much better rate than any of the other bondsman had agreed to. During the time we were dealing with her legal issues, he worked with her very kindly.

After I got her out, her first request to me was that I take her by some guy's house that she had been with when she was arrested. I questioned her as to why she would want to see him, and she stated that he had her telephone. I really tried to convince her that she shouldn't have anything more to do with him, but she insisted. As we drove over to his house, she told me how she just happened to be with him, having the meth, when they were pulled over by police. She said they let him go. I tried to explain to her that he was more than likely a snitch working for cops to keep from being arrested and the less she had to do with him, the better off she would be, but she still insisted on going by his house.

Okay, so she hadn't learned her lesson yet, so we went by there. I waited in the car while she went in. She told me she would only be a minute, but she was longer. I honked the horn, but she still didn't come out. I began backing out of the drive as she came out of the front door. I did not want to even be seen at a place where a known drug dealer/user was staying. As she got in the car, I began laying down some rules for her. I told her that there would be no more trips by a drug dealer's house under no uncertain circumstances. I told her that she would be staying at my house and she would get a job; the first time that I suspected that she was using drugs, I would put her on the street.

She got a job at a Mexican restaurant. She almost seemed like herself at times during the next week, until I received a telephone call from one of the DPS officers that I had worked with through the years. He began his conversation with an apology telling me that he had arrested my daughter for holding drug contraband. He asked me if I wanted to come and get her vehicle or I wanted him to impound it. My husband and I went to the location where he had stopped my daughter. She was in the patrol car. I asked him to get her out so I could talk to her. I then asked him to take off her handcuffs for a minute, and he did. I took my daughter's hands and stretched out her arms and examined them for needle marks.

As I looked at the fresh needle marks in her forearm, she tried to convince me the marks I was seeing were old ones. I just had to shake my head as I walked off away from her. I looked back as the officer was placing the handcuffs back on her and she was screaming at me to come and bail her out. I just kept walking and told her to figure it out for herself—a hard move for me but a good one. The bondsman that had bonded her in Taylor County came and bonded her out again. And she was back at my house. She was not allowed there unless my husband or I were there, and she was not allowed to have any friends there unless I knew them and knew they were drug-free.

My daughter was indicted in both Nolan and Taylor County for having drugs in her possession. She had to appear before the judge in Taylor County first. She couldn't afford an attorney, so she applied for one. I took her to see the judge when she turned in her paperwork for being indigent and unable to afford an attorney. God intervened the second time. While we were waiting to see the judge, I ran into an attorney that I knew through her being an ad item attorney for CPS. We talked briefly in the hallway, and she left. The judge invited me into his chambers as he spoke with my daughter. While I was sitting there, he asked me how I knew the attorney that I had been previously talking with. I explained that I had casually become acquainted with her through some CPS cases that I had worked. The judge told my daughter that he believed that I was a good person because of where I worked, and he told her he was assigning her a better attorney than he usually assigned.

When my daughter met with her attorney, he explained that there was a pretty solid case against her in Taylor County and that he believed that he could get Nolan County to merge their case in with Taylor County's case. This is what happened, and she pleaded guilty to a possession charge. She was sentenced to eight years of probation with fines and court costs. One of the conditions of her probation was that she go to drug treatment and attend AA meetings. The third time I believe God intervened was when she was assigned a probation officer. He was one whom I had worked with often through the years. He came to my office and told me that he was being assigned to my daughter, but before he accepted, he wanted to know how I felt about it.

I told him that I felt he would do whatever he felt is in the best interest for her and that I totally trusted him. He was a very good probation officer for her. He immediately got her into a drug treatment program in East Texas. As my husband and I drove her to the treatment facility, we all talked nervously. I told my daughter that this could be the change she needed in her life. It could be a new beginning from all of the past darkness that she had experienced. She would talk about it nervously because she really didn't know what to expect. After we got to the treatment facility, she was asked to leave all of her bags with the staff and say her goodbyes to us. Before we left, she was asked to provide a urinalysis. If she had any drugs in her system, she would not be allowed to stay. She was clean.

As I started to leave, she looked like that little girl that I sang to on my lap. She cried, and I cried. Although it was hard for me to leave her there, I knew it was for the best. It was the beginning of a long journey for her to get back home, back home to her own self, the daughter I knew. My husband hugged her and told her how proud of her he was because she had already tested clean on her first UA there. As he took my hand and we started out of the door, I blew her a kiss and tried not to let her see me cry. I don't know if the tears I shed that day were tears of relief, tears of joy, or tears of sadness because I had to leave my baby girl in a drug rehab, or just a combination of all of it, but I cried all the way home.

We were not able to see my daughter until the day she graduated from the drug rehab thirty days later. I remember as we drove to her graduation, I kept thinking to myself that thirty days was such a short time to get off of that drug. But much to my relief, she chose to stay and go to a halfway house where she could further get the treatment she needed. She told me that if she came back to where she had started using drugs, the same people would come around, and she feared that she would more than likely use again. I wholeheartedly supported her decision to stay and continue with treatment. For the first time since the nightmare of finding out that she was using meth, I saw a light that I used to see in my daughter's eyes. She had a hope and a longing for life inside her again, something that I could not have imagined seeing a year ago. I swelled with pride that day.

It has been seven years now since standing in that treatment facility. My daughter has not used meth since getting out. She has developed many meaningful relationships with people, she is now a mentor for those who are going into treatment programs, she has gotten her nursing license back, and she works full time for a neurologist. The fifth time that God intervened was when he gave my daughter her life back. I believe that God is an ever-interceding God, and that when you allow him to work, he will work.

My daughter became a Christian at a young age, and she has never stopped believing that God is God and that he is in control. She continues to look to him for guidance on a daily basis and has a very deep spiritual relationship with him, now more than ever. I have never given up on the fact that she would someday be my daughter again, and I knew that placing all of my trust in God would get us to that point. There is a song named "God of the Mountain." The song talks about God always being God in the valley of your life and on the mountain of your life; he certainly is the God of the Mountain, always there and interceding.

Kerrie Bullard and her Daughter

Kerrie Bullard with her Mother and Daughter

Chapter 13

When a child disappears into thin air, it is like something that no one can imagine. It is almost as if they were never there; only you know that they were. They left behind clothing, contact lenses, favorite CDs, a bedroom full of memorabilia, and family and friends who long to find them, people who had just spoken with them hours before they disappeared, who had shared precious times with them before they disappeared. How could a child be inside their own house, and the next few minutes, walk out the door and never be seen again?

When I received a call to investigate the case of a missing child in one of the counties I covered, I was a little overwhelmed. The case was already a month old and had grown very cold. I can't say why the other authorities had waited so long to contact our agency, but for some reason, they had failed to call us during the beginning stages of the case. I went directly to the police station and spoke with the chief of police. He told me that he suspected foul play in the case. He said the child had been missing for nearly a month, and the last person to see the child was the mother's paramour.

I remember the trip over to the home where the mother lived, where the child had also lived and was last seen. I had all of these thoughts going through my mind. What was this mom like? What kind of feelings was she experiencing? How would she perceive me being there? I wondered if she would answer any of the questions I had to ask. The chief of police accompanied me to the home where I met with the child's mother. I began the interview with her like all interviews—I began to ask her questions about herself to build a rapport. She was very courteous and polite. Much to my surprise, she was a very petite lady, a heavy smoker, and open to me being there. I recorded our conversation with her permission.

She told me that the last person to see her twelve-year-old daughter alive was her paramour. She said she had kicked him of the house, not because she suspected him of anything, but because he would not keep a job. Basically what had happened was she and the child's father had divorced. She had met this paramour, and he moved into her house with her. She said her daughter resented him because she always wanted her father and her to get back together, and her daughter looked at her paramour as being the one who kept them from getting back together.

I asked several other questions about some stuff that had been discovered in the home, such as some computer printouts about how to kill people, some devious looking masks and some videos that had been discovered on a computer. Her explanations were that she and her paramour had found it interesting about the different ways a person could be killed, but that didn't mean that she was looking for a way to kill her daughter. She said she just enjoyed reading this stuff. She said the masks were there because her paramour collected them, and the videos were of her paramour acting out a slasher film. She said it was just him and a cousin doing silly things.

There were over a thousand pages discovered in a closet that provided instructions and demonstrations of how to kill a person in different ways. In my mind, I thought that this was strange entertainment for someone, and even so, it didn't prove that anyone had killed this child. It just proved that someone was inquisitive about how to kill a person. The masks were those such as the one Michael Myers wore on *Friday the 13th* movie. This mom explained that her paramour collected these types of masks and that she had given them to him as gifts. There was a video of her paramour walking up behind an unsuspecting young man while that paramour was wearing the Michael Myers mask. The paramour had a machete and pretended to slit the throat of the unsuspecting man.

There were also gory videos that were made of this paramour and the same young man in the other video with a dead deer. They were hacking up the deer and talking about how much fun it was to kill the deer and hack it up. There was another video that showed the paramour smoking weed with the same man and acting high. I found out the young man in the videos was a cousin of the paramour. To me, these were certainly questionable but not proof that anyone had murdered this child. It just proved that this paramour had a very different kind of personality than most people do—one that I would not want any of my children around, especially alone, and that the mother apparently had a different view at some things than other mothers did.

The young missing girl had a brother who was sixteen at the time of her disappearance and also lived in the home. This mother had no concerns of her paramour harming her child and said that she totally trusted him. She said that during the time her daughter had disappeared, it was Christmas break. She said they had celebrated Christmas together with her paramour at his family's house in Big Spring, Texas. She said they had also stopped by her ex-husband's family's home and visited for a little while. On the day after, she said she went to work early that morning and saw her daughter in her bed asleep. She said that although she did not directly look at her, she knew it was her daughter. She said she didn't wake her or talk to her. The mom said she had agreed to allow her daughter to spend the night with one of her friends that night. She said her paramour told her that he saw her daughter as she walked out the door about 4:00 p.m. on December 26. He told her that the young girl said she was going to her father's house who lived in an apartment across the street and then to her friend's house who lived in Loraine, Texas.

Loraine, Texas is located about twelve miles from Colorado City, Texas, where this young girl's friend resided, and it was never really clear how the girl was going to get to her friend's house. According to the mom, someone in the girl's family was to pick up her daughter and give her a ride there. Once this young girl walked out of her house that day in December, she was never seen alive again. I spoke with some of this girl's friends at school who told me that she hated her mom's paramour and was deathly afraid of him. One of her best friends told me that when she spent the night at their home, the paramour could be seen underneath the doorway to the girl's room pacing back and forth in the hallway. She told me that the missing girl kept a baseball bat under her bed for protection.

When asked why she was afraid of the paramour, no one could really tell me a reason, just that she had stressed to them that she was very fearful of him. When I went into the young girl's bedroom, I observed it to be a very normal teenager's room. The walls were painted purple with her name stenciled on the walls. There were stuffed toys in the room, and her dressing table mirror had all of her friends' signatures that they had left on the mirror with cute little messages at some time or another when they had visited her. Some makeup, her contacts, her wallet, earrings, and other jewelry were on the table as well as her IPAD that she had gotten for Christmas. And the baseball bat was where her friend told me it would be. All of her clothing was in the room. Her mom guided me through the room and allowed me to photograph it.

I noticed that her door did not have a doorknob on it, and a scarf was tied through the hole where the doorknob had once been. Her mom said it had always been that way. According to her friends, they told me that the paramour used to peek into the hole and try to scare her at night. When I confronted the mother about this young lady's fears of her paramour and the baseball bat under the bed, she didn't believe it. She said her and her daughter always talked about things, and she believed that her daughter would have told her if she were afraid of her paramour. As for the bat, the mom said she loved to play baseball and during off season; she stored the bat there.

She was in total denial of the fact that her daughter could have been afraid of her paramour. In fact, the mom defended the paramour against anything negative that was said about him. I asked several times to interview him; however, he refused, stating his attorney would not allow him to be interviewed since he was being looked at by law enforcement as a person of interest. I spoke with the missing girl's brother who told me that he did not remember anything out of the ordinary leading up to the day she went missing. He said on the day she went missing, he came home and the door was locked, which was unusual. He said he beat on the door and rang the doorbell for about five to seven minutes. Finally his mom's paramour came to the door, stating that he did not hear the door and he had been in the bathroom. He said the paramour had dirt all over him and it looked like he had rolled in the dirt. He said the paramour told him that he had gotten that dirty at work and hadn't had a chance to get cleaned up yet.

He told me that he had not noticed his sister being fearful of the paramour, but she didn't like him much. The mom agreed to place her son with relatives until the case could be closed. During the time I was investigating this case, I met a very interesting lady whose daughter had been abducted and murdered in California. During the time we spoke, she told me that she believed the mom to be totally blinded by the paramour and that the paramour would more than likely be the one responsible for this child's disappearance. We kept in contact during the time I worked on the case by phone and sometimes in person.

The days turned into months, and the months turned into a year anniversary with no new leads. During the year preceding the child's disappearance, the mom was arrested twice. She was found to have had some prescription drugs with nothing to prove they were hers, and she hid the paramour from the police and hindered their investigation. As it turned out, she had allowed the paramour to continue to reside with her, and he had never moved out. The charges were eventually dropped on the mom. There were many vigils held for this young girl, and there was a lot of community support. One lady in the community came to me and told me that she had seen this young girl around 10:00 p.m. on the day she went missing. She said she knew the girl from seeing her around town. She said the young girl was standing near a local store with two other people——one being the girl she was supposed to have spent the night with. She said the other person appeared to be a boy who had been dating the missing girl's friend.

When the friend was questioned, she denied any knowledge of the girl ever having plans to spend the night with her, and she denied ever seeing her or her boyfriend that day. When the friend's boyfriend was questioned, he said he was working at Pizza Hut; however, the time cards showed he was absent from work that night. A search was done on her friend's home, but there was no trace of the missing girl ever being at her friend's home. As for her friend's boyfriend, he said he had lied to his employer about being sick and didn't want to get caught in the lie or lose his job. He said he was hanging out with his girlfriend when he was supposed to be at work.

The mom and her paramour decided to move to Austin, Texas, shortly after the girl disappeared. The mom explained that people would not leave her alone because she had chosen to be with her paramour even though he was a suspect in the disappearance of her daughter. Shortly after moving to Austin, Texas, she and her paramour broke up and went their separate ways. After breaking up, the mom held a news conference and stated that she did find out things about her paramour's personality that led her to believe that he could be involved in her daughter's disappearance.

On the day of my retirement, almost three years after she disappeared, this missing girl was found in a remote area in an adjoining county of where she went missing. She was near a place where the paramour had last worked, and she was deceased. I attended her memorial service. It was held in the high school gymnasium. There were a lot of people there. It was a sweet memorial to her. Her family and friends lined the gym floor. The local Bikers Against Child Abuse sat near the family. Many pictures of this child's life were shown in a slideshow. They were of happier times when her parents were living together and enjoying life, birthdays, Christmas times, and times with her friends.

This beautiful young girl would have been going into her senior year of high school this year. She would have been enjoying proms, dating, spending time with her friends, and all of the other things a girl her age would do. But someone took that away from her. As for the paramour, he had lied about where he was on the day this young girl went missing. He said he was at work all day, but it turned out that he had quit his job the day before. He said he lied because he thought the mom would be angry at him for quitting a good job.

The case still remains open and unsolved.

According to the mom, she had no knowledge that he had quit his job until after the girl went missing. But then again, for her to be so close to someone she lived with, this was just another time that she made blind excuses for him and herself. Everything in the case pointed in the direction of the paramour with the mom having knowledge of some things, but there just was not enough to get anything done. Again, I believe that one day in the final judgment, I can look across the floor of heaven as the murderer(s) of this young girl are judged, and maybe she will give me the beautiful smile that I looked at in all of her photographs as I got to know her during the investigation, and she will have the peace that she deserves. Until then, I know that she is in a place where no one can ever harm her again, and while that is no consolation to her murder, the thought is of some comfort.

Searcher for missing child with search dog

Tree lighting memorial one year after child went missing

Chapter 14

April 2, 2008

The trip to Lubbock, Texas, with my husband Jerry was a normal trip to the doctor for me. I was seeing a doctor about some pain that I had been having in my hand, and Jerry was seeing his skin doctor, so the trip served a dual purpose. I had already seen my doctor, set up an appointment for surgery on both hands for May 5, 2008, and had accompanied Jerry to see his doctor. While waiting for the doctor to come in, my phone rang. Much to my surprise, my supervisor was on the other end of the conversation. The reason it surprised me as much as it did was because when on medical leave while working for the state of Texas, your supervisor is not supposed to disturb you, so I chose to take the call because I felt it was probably very important.

He told me that the conversation would need to be held in the strictest of confidence because an operation with the state was going to play out in the next day or two. I excused myself from the room and walked out into the hallway and into a corner where there was no one else around to hear the conversation, and that's where I first heard of the FLDS compound in El Dorado, Texas. My supervisor told me of a ranch, (compound) located in El Dorado, Texas, where approximately one hundred fifty people were living; some of them children—young girls—who were reported being impregnated, sexually abused, and married by older men in the supposed religious sect.

He told me that I had been handpicked to join nine other investigators in raiding the compound to begin the investigation. He told me that this raid would more than likely take place on April 3, 2008, but he was not sure on this date and did not have a time for certain. He said that I would be receiving an e-mail instructing me when to leave the office and head in the direction of the San Angelo CPS office to meet up with the rest of the special investigators.

April 3, 2008, began like any other day as I went into the office. My supervisor who whose office was housed in Abilene, Texas, came into the office in Sweetwater, Texas, and waited with me until I received an e-mail about 3:00 p.m. on April 3, 2008, instructing me to head toward the San Angelo office. I remember as I left my office, I did it very quietly. The workers always had to sign out on a board their location of where they would be, and when I signed out on the sign-out board, I signed "If I tell you where I'm going, I'll have to kill you," and in the rerun back area I signed "Who knows when?" I put a smiley face beside it.

Before I could hit Highway 70 headed to San Angelo, I received a phone call from one of my close coworkers saying to me, "You are on a high-profile case, aren't you?" I told her that I couldn't talk about it, and she said that she understood and instructed me to be safe. My supervisor told me that I might be there in the San Angelo, Texas area a couple of days, so I needed to take a bag with me. I contemplated only packing for a couple of days, but then I began thinking about how difficult some children can be to interview, and if this were true—that children were being sexually abused—there may be some child removals. So I packed for a week, and I am glad that I did because the days turned into weeks and then months.

I followed my supervisor to the San Angelo, Texas CPS office where I met up with some investigators that I had never met before. At the time, I did not realize that these people would become my second family in a very short time. Out of the investigators who were going to be involved in the task force, six of us had been police officers in the past and were known as special investigators with the state agency. The others involved were regular investigators who were very experienced, and a couple of other supervisors from the San Angelo office.

We were all escorted to the El Dorado Community Center where we met with one of the San Angelo supervisors. I remember that he greeted me with "Hello, Kerrie. I hope this is all a false alarm" Make no mistake—this was no false alarm. But it didn't hurt to hope. Upon arrival at the community center, I remember noticing it was very scarcely furnished with a few folding chairs and a folding table. We were all shown some stuff that had been Googled regarding the FLDS religious sect—not a lot of information except that they did not like red because it symbolized evil, and they were very careful not to associate with people who were not of their FLDS religion. Unfortunately, I was wearing a red sweater, but it was nothing intentional. I had to separate myself from worrying about their beliefs and focus on what we as a team were going to do to protect these children.

This was also the first time I had even heard of the name Warren Jeffs. It seemed that he thought he was some type of a prophet and had a whole bunch of others believing that he was the Prophet and made every decision concerning their lives. He was the one who decided where they live, who they lived with, how much food they could have to eat, when they would be married and to whom they would be married, who would be kicked out of the FLDS sect, and anything else that had to do with them existing.

One other item we were shown before going into the compound was an aerial view of the compound itself. The ranch known as the Yearning for Zion Ranch was 1,700 square miles of land with some buildings on it. Very shortly after arriving at the El Dorado Community Center, we received a phone call that it was time to go to the FLDS ranch. It was now about 11:00 p.m. We left the community center and made the mile-and-a-half distance to the gates of the FLDS compound. Upon arrival, the gates were closed, and we were told that none of the men would be allowed into the compound; only the women investigators would be allowed to interview the children. We agreed to this, although I am not sure why this was agreed upon since there was a search warrant to enter the property and search for these children.

It was nearing midnight when the gates of the compound were opened. A car with me and three other ladies were allowed to enter with an FLDS member acting as our guide in the front leading vehicle and another vehicle with more FLDS people behind us. Once inside the gates, I looked back as the gates were being closed and locked. I remember looking at one of the ladies in the vehicle, who was one of the six of us who had been a police officer and who I had just met a few hours before, and telling her that we had just lost control of this situation. As long as they had the gates locked with us inside, we had no control. She agreed, and we both agreed that we would stay in contact with each other throughout the interview process.

It was pitch-dark throughout the compound except for this beautiful white building that was illuminated with lights. It appeared to be a vast building, larger than any building on the premises, appearing to stand taller than any other building. I remember thinking to myself, *What a beautiful church.* Or at least it appeared to be a church. The roads were winding, and it seemed like we drove for an eternity of twists and turns. I remember thinking to myself, *If I have to find my way out of here, head toward the church.* I didn't feel that I could find my way out if I had to, even using the "church" as a land marker because it seemed to be in the center of the compound to me. I wasn't sure that I would know where to go from there if I had to find my way out.

We finally arrived at our destination—a place that had been deemed by FLDS members as the place where we could meet with and interview the female children in the sect. It was the school. The building was constructed of logs that appeared to be handmade. As we entered the school building, I was filled with so many feelings: amazed at what I had seen, excited to find out what I could about the abuse, surprised at the things that I was seeing as I went inside the building, and wondering where this would lead. I can remember thinking to myself, *This looks larger than a one-hundred-fifty-person compound.*

As we climbed up the steps to the cabin-like school building, I noticed that both sides of the steps were lined with men who were modestly dressed in jeans and nicely starched and ironed pastel-colored shirts. Most of them had their hair combed similarly, short and parted to the side, and none of them, although they were polite, had smiles on their faces. And as we entered the building itself, I observed that the hallways were also lined with men on both sides of the wall. I immediately began to decipher that this was an intimidation tactic by them. I'm not sure why, but somehow I had gotten in with my laptop computer and camera. This was typical for me to have these items with me while interviewing children as it was state policy to photograph and record any interviews with children.

This was my first run-in with Mr. Merle Jessop. He did not like the idea of me photographing or recording the children, and Mr. Jessop began to tell me that I could not interview the children unless he was present. He told me that he had been left in charge by Warren

Jeffs. I guess that meant he was the "acting" Prophet. I explained to him that my job was to get a good interview, without the children being influenced by anyone, and it would be in his best interest not to interfere. He politely stepped aside and allowed me to proceed to one of the upstairs classrooms where I met the others from the San Angelo office. I met investigators from the San Angelo office and a female supervisor from San Angelo.

Much to my surprise, these women had tried to mimic the ladies of the compound by dressing similarly to them. None of them were wearing makeup and had on very long dresses or skirts, no jewelry, and looked very plain. I later learned as I worked alongside these ladies that this way of dressing was not typical for them, but they explained that they had hoped to get in good favor or gain trust by dressing this way. And here I was with red fingernails, lots of jewelry, and a red sweater, not to mention that I had already had a run-in with the man left in charge! I thought to myself, *Way to go, Kerrie.*

During this short debriefing from the female San Angelo supervisor, we were told that an intake had been received by a young girl named Sarah Barlow, who claimed to be living on the compound. She reported that she was pregnant and had been forced to marry an older man on the compound. We were told this girl was able to describe the temple (the church I had seen as we came in), the interior of the buildings, and some of the people in the compound.

We each went into classrooms to begin our interviews. The rooms were furnished with desks and had a large framed photo of Warren Jeffs on the wall as well as photos of who I later learned were past Prophets of the FLDS, to include Rulon Jeffs, Warren Jeff's father who had preceded Warren Jeffs as the prophet until his death. It was arranged nearly like the public school classrooms, but instead of Presidents' photographs, there were the past Prophets' photos. The books were also very different than normal school books and spoke more of FLDS rules and history.

I found it hard to fathom what I was in for during the next several hours of interviewing. I had already noticed that things were being done very differently than normal policy and procedures, with us allowing them to lock us behind gates, taking us to a location of their choosing for interviews, no male investigators being allowed into the compound with us, and none of the other investigators having a laptop or a camera.

Although the other investigators had their cell phones, for some reason, mine was the only one that seemed to work well in the compound.

Finally the interviewing began, and it was then that I realized not only were the men lining the hallways were meant as an intimidating tactic for us as the investigators, it was also meant for these children we were going to interview. As we began to get them for interviews, the children were paraded from a room in the back of the school, down through the hallways lined by these men, and into the classroom where they would be interviewed. Normally, you wouldn't think that was why these men were there; you would think that maybe it's their father trying to make sure they were okay, but that was not their intent.

Going into this, I think that everyone from the outside were thinking of this group as a religious group, not some group who had been breaking the law. I'm not really sure what everyone's thoughts were, but I do know this for certain: things were not being done like policy and Texas laws said they should be done, and there were many allowances being made for this group of people. I do remember hearing someone say that the law enforcement people did not want to see another Waco or Ruby Ridge incident in this investigation, and that is why such care was being taken in how this was done.

I also kept thinking to myself that even though I could not see a lot as we were coming in, the "church" was such a large church for only one hundred fifty people to be housed in that compound. I made a call to my supervisor on the outside and let him know that I felt there was more to this than what everyone was telling us; furthermore, I felt there were more people on this compound than we were being told. He then instructed me that he felt that it would be necessary to send in a second wave of investigators to help with the interviewing and relieve us by morning.

I was not prepared for what I would see in the first child that I interviewed. She was dressed in a long pastel dress, long sleeves, and her hair was long and French-braided in pigtails. Other than looking like a child dressed in clothing from the 1800s, she appeared healthy. She did not smile, and her answers to my questions were very short and simple. She was small in stature and spoke very politely and softly. She looked to be about seven years old and told me that she was six.

When I tried to establish a rapport by asking questions like what do you like to do for fun, she answered with "Clean." I asked her what she liked to clean, and she would say "The house and yard." What do you want to be when you grow up? "A good mother and a good wife." What kind of toys do you like to play with? "Toys are idols and not allowed." What do you learn in school? "We learn to be good mothers and how to take care of our houses and children." "We learn about the Prophet and what he wants." Who told you that toys are idols? "The Prophet." Who is the Prophet? "Rulon Jeffs and Warren Jeffs." These were typical answers that I received for most of my interviews. It was almost as if I was talking to robots.

When the children were asked about sexual abuse, physical abuse, or neglect, they all gave the same answer: "My mother is a good mother who was taught by the Prophet to obey the rules." The next child in for an interview looked like the other one I had just finished with, and the next, and the next, and so on. I eventually began going back through my camera, looking at the pictures of the children I had interviewed; it was then that I realized that the men of the FLDS were ushering in the same children over and over. We were interviewing the same children.

I went to the other lady investigator who had been a police officer and showed her some of the pictures that I had taken, and she agreed. It was then that we caught the men of the FLDS hustling the girls from one interviewer to another, the same little girls over and over. We met up again with the lady San Angelo supervisor and the other investigators and told them what we thought was happening. At that time, an administrative assistant from the San Angelo office was brought in, and she began monitoring the children who were being brought out to interview.

At some point, this administrative assistant began smelling burning paper. It was then that she discovered that some of the women of the compound were shredding some papers in another room close by. We later found out the papers would turn out to be very important documentation that would blow this case wide open—diaries that had been kept by some of the children on the compound describing their marriages or being chosen by the prophet to be "spiritually united" with whoever the Prophet had chosen for them.

The night was a long night of getting no results from the girls we had interviewed. The older ones were not cooperative, and the younger ones, although polite, did not provide any information. Mr. Jessop had instructed the members of the compound to be polite but not to allow us to use any of their facilities. We were not offered anything to drink. Eventually, I found myself in confrontation with Mr. Jessop again. I explained to him that we were human and needed to be allowed access to their facilities. I was told that because we were not of their faith, we would defile their facilities. I explained to him that it was either defile their facilities or their floors. He agreed to allow us to use the facilities.

At around 7:00 a.m., I received a phone call from my supervisor. He asked if any of the food or drinks they had sent in had been delivered to us, and I explained they had not. He said that he had sent in food and drinks about an hour earlier. I found myself in confrontation with Mr. Jessop. He said that nothing would be allowed in from the outside and that we could not leave the premises without being completed with our interviews and investigation. I asked him directly if he was holding us against our will, and I explained this as being a felony since it is considered kidnapping. I also explained to him that some of us had medical needs and needed to be able to get to our medications, which were in our vehicles outside of the locked gates. I am an insulin-dependent diabetic and desperately needed to get to my insulin.

He then agreed to allow three of us to leave the compound, telling us that we could return on to the premises after a short break. I called my supervisor and told him what had transpired and that some of us would be coming out shortly for a short break. By now, it was light outside and April 4, 2008. As we walked out of the school building, I was stunned at what I saw. There were many houses—large houses, two- and three-story houses—built out of the same log cabin wood. There were more than I could count. There were also large buildings all over the place, not to mention what looked like a sewer system and a rock or gravel pit. And next to that large temple was another smaller one. I knew at this time that there were more than one hundred fifty people on this compound.

Just like when we went in, we were escorted out by a car in front of us as well as one behind us. As we left the gated area, I saw that there was a guard tower near the gates. I had not noticed this before until now. I wondered if there was anyone on the compound with a weapon. Once outside of the gates, we were able to meet with the male investigators and supervisors as well as some Texas rangers and other law enforcement who had gathered. We told them what we suspected: that there were more people on the compound than we were told and that we were not having any luck getting anyone to be truthful and forthcoming about the one who had reported this incident or about any girls being married to or impregnated by older men in the compound. We also notified the Texas rangers about the diaries that confirmed young girls being spiritually united with men in the compound.

April 4, 2008

We made our way to a convenience store in town where I got a diet Coke and some sort of stale sandwich. As we turned the corner off the dirt road that led to the compound on to the pavement leading to town, I noticed that CNN was setting up a mobile unit. I knew that the story was about to be broadcast and that my family would soon be learning about where I was. I called my husband from the store and told him that I felt that he would be learning very quickly about this investigation on national television. I told him that I was fine and not to worry and to contact my parents and let them know that everything was okay.

He later told me that when he called my mom, she had immediately told him that she suspected that I was in El Dorado once she heard the news about the raid. My mom just knew. She has always known things about me when I didn't think that she did. In a couple of hours, we were back at the compound. This time, we were accompanied in by the Texas rangers and some other law enforcement as we entered. We were instructed by Texas rangers that we would be going from cabin to cabin to search the premises for children under the age of seventeen. I was amazed at the fact that portable toilets were being brought in, some grills and coolers with drinks were brought in and were being set up. It was almost like going to a state fair. The place was now alive and no longer quiet as it had been the night before. There were police, Texas Rangers, and DPS troopers everywhere.

I had once watched a movie called the *Sugarland Express*. This reminded me of that movie. Cops were coming from under the woodwork, it seemed! As we began our house by house search, it was becoming very evident that these people were less than honest and that there were more than one hundred fifty people on the compound. I observed as they took pictures of us. I was still in my red sweater, and later I saw my picture as I was going up the steps to a house. I was labeled by them as the Gestapo!

At some time in the afternoon, we were told that the judge had ordered the removal of all children eighteen years and younger and for them to be taken to the community center. But as time would tell, the community center was not large enough to hold the children that were removed. Now not only CNN was covering the story but just about every national news cast was covering it. Everywhere I looked, there were cameras, including the FLDS people taking videos and photographs. I didn't care what they had labeled me; I was there to make sure these children were safe and they were not being abused in any way.

As far as a second wave of investigators coming in to help, that had not happened yet, but at least now the men investigators and the law enforcement were on the grounds and going through the buildings with us. The houses were beautifully built with much care. According to some of the FLDS people, the men had been handpicked by Warren Jeffs to construct and build each of the buildings in the compound, and only certain people had been chosen to reside there because this is the holiest of all of the compounds of FLDS. According to the people residing there, this was the only compound that housed a temple.

The people of FLDS would lead everyone to believe that they had no knowledge of the outer world because they kept to themselves, but once inside their houses, it was very apparent that they had every modern convenience to include computers, satellites, cell phones, newer model vehicles, and very nice kitchens that were built somewhat like kitchens seen in restaurants. The houses had wall-to-wall carpet, grand pianos, and were neatly kept, which was very surprising because of the amount of people living in the homes. It appeared that one to two families occupied at least one of the floors.

In each of the families, there were anywhere from five and above mothers in the home; in other words, multiple wives for the man of the house. Each of the children addressed all of the women as mother, and each of the women took on the role of caring for the children and taking care of the household. It appeared that the children did not really know who their biological mother was, but to them, all of the women in the home were called mother.

Interestingly enough, while going through the homes, we did learn that there were some very young-looking women in the homes either pregnant or caring for children they called their own. Then finally, more CPS workers from all over the state of Texas started showing up to help. Some were a big help, and some had to be escorted off the property because they did not follow rules and kind of looked at this as "being their big break" or something to get attention. They did not take it very seriously. At some point, busses were brought in, and the first wave of females that we believed was between the ages of twelve and seventeen were escorted to the community center to be interviewed.

We went back to the community center where the sheriff met us and agreed to get those girls asking if he could get them something to eat. They told him that they wanted cheeseburger and milkshakes. That's what he gave them, and although you wouldn't believe that people would use food to create a distraction, they did. These people are only used to eating the food they produce naturally and not processed food; therefore, they became ill by just eating one meal of greasy hamburger meat and dairy products full of fat. They began to throw up and became violently ill. I remember seeing them laughing among themselves as they ordered the food. They knew exactly what they were doing. In my opinion, they were very deceptive. Maybe they had been taught to be this way, but they were old enough to know right from wrong.

This in itself created a stir, and the community came out to help by bringing fresh vegetables and fruit to the children, and nothing processed. I could not believe the amount of food that showed up in that place in just a matter of a few hours. People were beginning to feel sorry for them and look at us as if we were doing bad things to them. I could not fathom idolizing a person the way these people appeared to be worshiping Warren Jeffs. They were very protective of him and really believed that he was the prophet.

The community center had gone from being an empty building with very few items in it to a place where cots were set up. The community organizations like churches were coming in to help with food items, and by now others from CPS were starting to arrive, especially people like administrative directors, other program directors, and the regional director. It was finally dawning on people that the ten of us alone could not handle all of this; however, because we had gathered a vast amount of information, we were deemed as being the task force for this project and in-charge of the investigation for CPS.

Just from the information we were beginning to gather, the judge decided that all of the children would be removed and taken to the local coliseum and to the old army bunkers near the CPS office. It was also decided that because of their religion being so different from any other we had dealt with, the mothers could accompany the children. I wasn't really sure who had decided this.

This was way beyond the realm of policy for the state because even though some of the children were very young, the mothers were also considered as perpetrators because they had knowledge of the sexual abuse that was going on between the men and the younger girls. Moreover, some of the pictures that we had gathered had the mothers' pictures, participating in the spiritual union.

We found ourselves back on the compound with law enforcement and the Texas rangers going from house to house, collecting children, and placing them on school and church busses that were loaned to us so the children and their mothers could be moved to either the coliseum or the old army barracks at Fort Concho. It was a long day, but FLDS had become more cooperative and were waiting for us as we entered each home and collected the children, taking them to the busses. Other people from CPS began to help with the care of the children and the mothers by monitoring, being available for any of their needs, and anything else that might be needed.

We, the ten of us, continued with interviews of the children. In the end, three hundred sixty-seven children were removed—the largest removal of children believed to have occurred in the history of the United States. It seemed like a total chaos at some times, and I wondered how we would get through this. Lots of staff to include doctors and nurses was brought in. The children were examined and DNA tested to match them with their biological parents. DNA samples were taken from the mothers of the compound, and once the mother named who the father of the child was, a DNA sample was taken from him. The mother was not always cooperative; we had to rummage through the records in an attempt to find out who certain parents were. The records that were collected in the school proved to be very good information as a lot of the marriage certificates and birth records were located on these children.

The one thing that I can say for the FLDS was that they were certainly good about recording events. Some of the photographs we found were photos taken after the death of one of the male FLDS members. The body would be posed in the casket and the wives of that particular person would be posed standing near and around the casket. It almost looked like a family portrait.

Information we were gathering not only included birth records and marriage records but also pictures and audible recordings of events taking place. It seemed that this FLDS sect recorded everything to include marriages, births, deaths, and the plans for this FLDS compound. Although records indicated that the children were being taught history, the history they were being taught was the history of FLDS. The children could read and write but did not appear to know a lot about the outside world itself as far as historical events etcetra.

I was asked to interview a woman who had escaped from FLDS. She had escaped from the FLDS compound in Arizona after being forced to marry her cousin. She had four children with him. One of the children chose to stay on the compound, and she was still heartbroken about that, wondering if her child was one of the ones who had been married off to an older person. She had no idea where her child could be located. She told me that although she did not hold true to the FLDS beliefs, she could understand why the children and other wives would not be cooperative. She said they were more than likely fearful of what would happen if anyone were to ever find out they told any of the truth.

She told me that although she no longer is a part of the sect, she holds many fond memories of her own biological family. She told me that her parents are not allowed to have contact with her even though she knows within her heart that they still love her. She stated that her younger sister had married Rulon Jeffs, Warren Jeff's father, but Rulon had since died. She told me that Rulon was the Prophet before he passed away and that Warren Jeffs had somehow stolen the position of prophet from his older brother. She told me that Warren Jeffs is a very dishonest person. She said that in the earlier days, they all lived in a place called Short Creek. She said they had lived in normal housing and neighborhoods and that Warren Jeffs was the principal of the school. She said that there were rumors that he had molested some of the children during that time, and he used his position in the school to gain power. She said he was the favorite of Rulon Jeffs' sons.

She told me that Rulon Jeffs began having strokes, and Warren Jeffs had kept him separated from the rest of the sect by stating that Rulon had chosen him to be his messenger. By the time that Rulon Jeffs passed away, Warren Jeffs had appointed himself as the Prophet. He declared that no one but him could marry Rulon's wives, and he did. She stated her sister escaped him by running away from the sect. She said that things went from bad to worse, and the FLDS parishioners were made to reside in compounded neighborhoods and the children's toys and pets were taken away because Warren Jeffs declared them as idols.

April 5, 2008

Attempts had been made to get cooperation from FLDS to allow access into the temple to search. The temple was the only building that had not been entered, and Sarah Barlow the one who had reported and caused this investigation to begin had not yet been located. According to FLDS, if we went inside, the building would be defiled and they could no longer use it as their temple; however, we had to get inside to gain access to attempt to locate Sarah Barlow. Texas Rangers used force to gain entry to the FLDS temple. The building was a vast building, looking something like a church building. It was built of pure white hand-masoned stone. Although the building was a beautiful building, it was not used for beautiful things.

Records were obtained from the vault in the temple, and a room was discovered in the temple that no of us one had ever imagined would be in there. However the lady that I had spoken with stated that a room such as this had been in the plans for a long time, and she had hear talk of this room. The room contained white bedding and three chairs. As it turned out, through searches of the records, this room was used to train the young brides to be sexually active with their husbands. The chairs were for Warren Jeffs, and some his higher-ups, to observe and instruct. In other words, Warren Jeffs was using his religion to be sexually active with young girls and to be involved in the commission of sexual abuse.

As it turned out, there really was no Sarah Barlow, or at least she was never found. There was a young lady who claimed to be the one who called in the CPS intake that started this whole investigation; however, she had mental problems and was not held accountable for making the false report. By now, a room had been developed for the CPS task force to use so that evidence could be sorted through and records could be read for evidence. There was so much evidence that had been gathered that the investigation continued.

There was one audio tape that had been located in the vault of the temple that would send chills throughout you: the voice of a very young twelve-year-old child who Warren Jeffs was training to be a good wife. As I write this, I can still hear the voice of that child as Warren Jeffs violated her sexually.

Most of the children had been interviewed, and a decision had been made that the children would be placed into foster group homes. Charter busses were obtained, and the children were sectioned off into age groups. Extra help from all over the state was sought out, and this staff rode with the different children on the busses. During the interviews, the children kept referring to the raid that had taken place in Short Creek in the 1940s and this raid being just like it. They said they had been taught about it in history, and they were warned that it would happen again. They claimed this was a part of their prophecy.

It appeared that during this particular raid, all of the men in the FLDS sect were rounded up and arrested, being accused of bigamy. There were no accusations of sexual abuse during this raid. By this time, there were DPS staff involved, the Texas Ranger staff, other law enforcement agencies involved, and CPS staff from all over the state. As for the original ten, we were still working in our room at the CPS office in San Angelo Monday through Friday. Those of us who did not live in San Angelo continued to stay at the Stay Bridge Inn and Suites during the week. We would go home on the weekends.

This case had gone further than anyone could have ever imagined. We had gone from having ten CPS investigators to having hundreds or thousands of CPS workers, three hundred sixty-seven children, DPS troopers, Texas Rangers, doctors, nurses, attorneys, and whoever else that had been brought in to help. I cannot imagine the cost of this investigation, but I have heard that it was in the millions of dollars. We named our working room at the San Angelo CPS office "The War Room." It served its purpose well as that for us because that is where we as a team went to war for these children, trying to make sure that they would never have to return to the situations they had been a part of.

By now, the days were beginning to run together, and I was beginning to lose track of what day it was. At night, when I slept, the names of the children would go through my mind over and over. I thought of what they had been through and this child that had called in the report had not yet been found. I knew that in the end, something of this monstrosity we called a case would eventually make sense. Or would it? Was there really a Sarah Barlow, or was there this crazy woman that somehow knew enough to make this report that would eventually capture and cause Warren Jeffs to be in prison the rest of his natural life?

We were reading through piles and piles of paperwork, listening to recordings, and looking at photograph after photograph of young brides with wide smiles as they stood next to the man they had just married, some of the men as many as thirty to forty years older than these children. This was unlike something I had never imagined in my life. There was nothing normal about this, and certainly something that no child should ever be smiling about. But at the end of the day, everything was somewhat neatly tucked away, and those of us who stayed in the hotel went to our hotel—a place that we soon began to call home away from home, the Stay Bridge Inn. This is where we ate dinner together, reminisced through what we had learned during the day, talked about our families, and shared more about our lives than most coworkers do; after all, we were all living under the same roof.

By now, I had realized that I was not going to be able to keep the hand surgery appointments, so I cancelled them until I would be through with this case. Every day began with discussion of what we had located or discovered from the day before, and then we moved on to another box of records. File after file, page after page, paragraph after paragraph—an endless mountain, it seemed. By now, we had brought in case history experts who could rummage through and make sense of what child belonged in what person list, and birthdates, names, social security numbers, etc. were entered by those case history experts. So our ten became twelve, and then a state attorney room became the second room occupied by state legal staff. These were the attorneys who were filing our suits, going to court for us, and helping us with any legal needs. Our CPS family who was once only ten was beginning to grow again.

Warren Jeffs had been detained in Arizona on similar charges, but before being detained, we found records of his travels all over the United States while evading police and arrest. He was accompanied by what he called his scribe, Naomi. She was responsible for keeping his records of what he was doing during their travels. I had begun to know this man quite well. It's amazing to me that one day you are sitting in a doctor's office, and in just a phone call, everything changes. You begin to know people that you have never heard of before or met before, even if you never meet them face to face.

The ramblings that we read were constant. He would talk about dreams he had that directed him to do certain things, like excommunicate one of the men in the sect, or take someone's children and give them to another man, telling the children, "This is now your father." It was a constant tangle of a mess, and everyone in the sect just accepted it, believing this was the wishes of their Prophet. He had a mesmerizing power over these people that I could not understand. His followers were very devout and did anything and everything he asked, even on the run from the law. He always had plenty of money delivered to him, clothing, and cars. He did travel in style, mostly in Escalades.

After many months of reading through letters, birth records, death records, and listening to audio tapes, we had gathered enough evidence to say that there was enough evidence to prove that Warren Jeffs was responsible for marrying and having sexual relations with several young girls, the youngest being twelve years old and the daughter of none other than Mr. Merle Jessop, my good friend! The photograph that I saw of Warren Jeffs with this young girl was something that no one could ever imagine seeing or forget seeing. It was almost indescribable and sickening, but it very definitely confirmed the fact that Warren Jeffs had done something that no one should ever be allowed to do—marry a child. The picture will be forever branded in my mind.

The audio tape that we had earlier discovered fit well with this photograph and made the evidence itself intertwine. Both this tape as well as the photograph became nationally known to news media. Although the young girl's face was never shown, I had seen it in person when we removed her from the compound and on the picture when we discovered it. Although we had worked very hard to make the removals of these young girls stick, the state eventually agreed that if the mothers of the children would sign safety plans stating that none of the known sexual perpetrators would be allowed near the children, even if the perpetrator was the child's biological father, and that the mother would take a specialized parenting class that included education on protection as well as sexual abuse education, the children would be returned.

All of the children, with the exception of the twelve-year-old wife of Warren Jeffs that had become so nationally known, were returned to their mother. This particular child was allowed to remain in the care of family members who were not associated with the FLDS sect. So many people were involved in the case making decisions, including the Governor, that not all of the usual policies of CPS were followed and exceptions were made. This made it appear that everything the task force had done to protect these children was for nothing, and many of us came away with a feeling of anger—feelings that we were victims ourselves, feelings that our system had let us down, but mostly feelings that we had let these children down.

Some people say that when you go to war, you sometimes come back with nightmares, sleeplessness, and sometimes the person is not the same as they were before they left for war. I think I can honestly say that for each of us who were there in that task force day in and day out; we will forever be changed because of this experience. These essentially religious people were not really religious. They were a cult of sorts with very sick and unconstitutional beliefs. They were not victims as they tried to portray to the media and anyone else who they could get to listen to them. They were very dishonest and used their religion to be dishonest and get away with it.

What I came away with was that the FLDS sect was a group of people that had broken off from the Mormons. In the beginning, they lived a somewhat normal life, living in regular neighborhoods, children playing with toys, having pets, and attending public schools. As life went on, things began to change for the sect in that they became more segregated in a compound, toys and pets were taken from the children, and multiple-wife marriages were recognized as their religious belief. According to their belief, the more wives a man had, the closer to heaven he would be.

As life moved into the nineties for this sect, Warren Jeffs was allowed more access to the children, being the school principal. And by now, the children were no longer attending public schools because the sect did not want them influenced by the public. In the late nineties, Warren Jeffs became more controlling than ever as his father, Rulon Jeffs, fell ill and eventually had a fatal stroke. Before his death, Warren began to deliver messages to the sect stating his father had instructed him to deliver these messages to them, and they believed it.

He would make changes in their beliefs, outcast certain male members of the sect who he felt would be a threat to him, and give their wives and children to other men. He never told the congregation that his father was as ill as he was; he just said that his father had chosen him to deliver these messages to them. When Rulon Jeffs passed away, Warren convinced the congregation that he had been told by Rulon that he was to be the next Prophet, and that is when things drastically changed for the sect. It was believed that the younger and purer the bride, the closer to heaven a man would be, taking his tribe of wives with him. The more wives, the better for the men, and the women felt honored they were chosen because surely this would guarantee their entrance into heaven.

The age for marrying went from eighteen to no limit of how young. By now, the generations had changed from knowing what they had learned in the earlier days to what they were now learning. Their beliefs were changed, and all they knew was what their Prophet Warren Jeffs was teaching them. In the mid-2000s, Warren Jeffs decided to construct the Yearning for Zion (YFZ) Ranch located in El Dorado, Texas. The land, 1,700 acres, was purchased, and the construction began. Anyone who was chosen to live on the YFZ was privileged.

The ranch was a special one because out of the compounds the FLDS families resided on, this was the only one that would house a temple on it. Those who were chosen by Warren Jeffs to help with the construction of the ranch were privileged, even if they were not going to be a part of the residing community. Everything on the ranch was hand-constructed from their rock quarry and from their lumber mills. The ranch itself not only housed many three-story log cabins but a large storage facility where materials for clothing, canned food items (canned by the women of the compound), vegetables from the gardens, and any other items needed to take care of the congregation. There was also a self-contained sewer system, trucking station, and a rock quarry.

The congregation took care of their own needs mainly without help from the outside. According to the locals in El Dorado, one or two of the congregation members would be sometimes seen in town, but very rarely. The women and children all wore homemade pastels that covered them from neck to feet, and their undergarments covered their arms, midsection, and legs. The undergarment was called a holy garment and was never removed totally, even when bathing. The men mostly wore pastel or denim shirts and blue jeans, but I also noticed that they wore Oakley brand sunglasses and caps.

The vehicles consisted of newer model pickups, vans, or SUVs, some being Cadillac Escalades with satellites on them. All in all, other than having some different beliefs, these people were not as backwoodsy as some would believe upon first glance. They were as modern as the world is and had knowledge of computers and the government as a whole but attempted to play dumb to these things. They were taught to be totally dishonest.

During the months that I spent working on the El Dorado project, my father who had been very ill became worse. I would come home on weekends, spend time with my own family, and return to San Angelo during the week, staying at the Stay Bridge Inn & Suites. When Sunday afternoons came around, on my way out of town I would stop by to see my mom and dad. Dad would always ask the same question, "Are you going to be working in San Angelo this week?" And I would always answer him with, "Yes, Dad, that's where I'll be".

It was the weekend before the first of the trials was to begin. On August 16, 2008, I cooked a birthday meal for my dad, and we celebrated his eighty-second birthday with him and Mom, joined by my husband and sister for a desert of homemade banana pudding. My dad had asked me to make some fried pork chops, mashed potatoes, gravy, and asparagus for him. I had asked him if he would like a cake, and he requested the banana pudding. We had a good celebration, and Dad seemed to enjoy it.

I left town for San Angelo on August 18, 2008, but before leaving, I stopped by mom and dad's house as usual. It was a little more different this time, as Dad was sleeping when I arrived. He slept the whole time I was there, and I told my mom that I wouldn't disturb him. But Mom told me that he would be disappointed if I didn't say good-bye to him. I went quietly into his room and peeked in. My dad didn't ask me anything like he usually did, but he gave me the sweetest smile, and I told him that I was leaving for San Angelo and would see him when I returned. I hugged him and told him that I loved him very much, and I left. He didn't say anything.

I slept very soundly that night until I woke up around 3:00 a.m. after having a dream that my mom had called me, sobbing, saying that Dad had passed away. It seemed to be so real, but as I sat up and looked around, I could see that I was in my suite at the Stay Bridge. I didn't go back to sleep. I was anxious about the trial's beginning, and then this dream. It was a very long night after that.

On August 19, 2008, I was in the court room waiting as the trials had just began when I was approached by a lady who said she was the district clerk. She told me that she had an emergency phone call for me. I knew that it was news about my dad. As I walked into her office, she showed me where I could go to take the call privately. My husband was on the other end of the phone. He said that my dad had gone into a coma, and he felt that I should come home right away. My dad was on hospice, so they had already been called. I took a deep breath, trying not to fall apart, and told him to go to Daddy and tell him that I was on my way home, to please wait on me. I asked him to stay with my mom until my sister could get there.

As I drove the seventy-eight miles back home, I prayed that God would just give me one more conversation with my dad. I prayed that prayer over and over as I drove home. That is all I really remember about the drive home: me praying. I got to my mom and dad's house, and my dad was awake in his recliner. He was weak and not very alert. My husband told me that when he had told my dad to wait on me, my dad opened his eyes and asked him to help in getting into his chair.

As I spoke to my dad, he looked at me like he was glad to see me. But he didn't speak, just gave me an expression that made me know that he knew that I was there. He was choking, and my sister was helping him. She told me that he was in congestive heart failure and that fluids were beginning to build up. My sister is a nurse, and she was administering some of his medications. She had tried to give him some tea to drink, but he would choke as he tried to swallow.

I got a straw and got some of the tea—like I used to do with my children when they were infants—and began giving him a little bit at a time. It seemed to work pretty well, although he would strangle from time to time. Mom and I talked and decided that I should call his brother and sister and tell them he was not doing well. I called, and they came right away.

I was sitting in the chair next to my dad, holding his hand, when I asked his if he knew how much I loved him. There was a lot going on with the family being there, and all of the talking between them all. But I heard my dad as, in his very frail sentences, in a voice that I could barely hear, he asked me if I knew how much he loved me. It took me a minute to decipher what he had said, but I knew that it would not be long until he graduated into heaven. I nodded to him and squeezed his hand. I couldn't talk. I could hardly breathe. My dad was dying, and I couldn't do anything to stop it. All I could do was wait with him.

His sister and brother left that night, knowing that they would not see my dad alive again. It must have been so hard for them. For as long as I have lived, I have never seen them so emotionally drawn. I heard my uncle sobbing as he walked away from the house. By now, Dad was restless but was not saying anything. I sat beside him, quietly holding his hand and reassuring him that I would be there with him no matter what. My mom told him that it was okay to let go and be in heaven because he had lived a good, full life. My sister sat on the other side of him for a while and talked gently to him, reassuring him that she loved him and what a good father he had been.

In a while, my mom asked me if it would be okay for her to rest a while, and I told her that I would stay with Daddy. My sister had worked a night shift the night before and had been up with Dad for the most part of the day, so she was exhausted. I told her that she should rest if she felt like she needed to, and she did. I sat with Dad for several hours, holding his hand and reassuring him that I was there. I gave him morphine drops as he needed them on a regular basis.

At about 3:00 a.m., Dad began to struggle with choking on his own fluids, so I awakened my sister. We decided that it was time to call the hospice nurse again. She told us that we should increase his morphine dosage and she would be there as soon as she could go by the supply room to pick up some things. My sister and I sat by Dad, helpless except for just soothing him as much as we could with what we had. I know that it was a struggle for him because he moaned very often until I would rub his hand and talk to him, and he would get quiet.

He began to go into Cheyne–Stokes respiration, a breathing pattern that most people who are dying go into just before death. That's when I woke my mom up and told her that she probably needed to be near Dad. My dad took his last breath while I was holding his hand, talking to him, and my mom and sister were standing nearby and talking to him. We all wished him a well trip into heaven and told him that we would see him again one day. Because my dad had suffered with Parkinson's disease, his jawline and mouth always appeared so clenched to the point that he always looked so unhappy. As my dad took his last breath, I saw such a peaceful look on his face. I had not seen my dad look like that in years. His jaw and mouth were no longer clenched; in fact, he had a smile on his lips.

They say that when God speaks, you hear him. I heard him that morning telling me that Dad was okay. The hospice lady arrived about twenty minutes after Dad passed away. She had taken three hours to get to Mom and Dad's house from Abilene, which is about forty miles away. I was not at all pleased with her and asked her to do what she had to get done and leave. My dad's favorite song was "The Unclouded Day." When I would play the piano for Mom and Dad, he would always ask me to play that song for him. And when I would sing specials for his Sunday school class in earlier days, he would ask me to sing that song.

I wanted to do something special for Dad's flower arrangement, so Mom and I made the trip down FM 419 into Fisher County to my grandparent's old farm where Dad had been raised. From the gateposts, I took some of the wood to make a cross. While I was collecting it, my mom who was waiting in the car motioned for me to come to the car. As I opened the door to see what she wanted, I saw tears in her eyes; "The Unclouded Day" was playing on the radio. I think my dad was telling us that he is okay.

I took the wood I had collected from the gates to my grandparent's farm, and my husband fashioned a cross that was placed in the flower arrangement with a ribbon saying "Daddy's Home." I removed this after the funeral and the cross hangs on my wall near my piano and near my dad's picture. After a week had passed, I returned to San Angelo and the same old routine of reading and getting information for the trials.

I was eventually sent to San Antonio, Texas, again to interview a young sixteen-year-old who had given birth to a baby fathered by a forty-two-year-old man. Once we finally found this young girl and she produced a baby, DNA evidence was taken. Upon getting the results, the baby she produced was not even hers. Another example of how dishonest the people of the FLDS were. We were never able to find that baby, and a warrant was issued for the young girl because she had interfered with an investigation. Who knows if it will ever be served, or if she will ever spend time in prison? She was from Canada and may have returned there.

This was just another example of the control Warren Jeffs had over these people. He had summoned her parents, who were Canadian FLDS members, to send their daughter to the YFZ ranch to be married to one of the men who resided there. They followed his directions. Although it is hard to fathom anyone doing such a thing, it happened. Eventually, Warren Jeffs, Merle Jessop, and several others of the FLDS men were indicted on several counts of child abuse and sexual abuse. Some made plea deals, and some fought. Those who made pea deals got sixty years. Those who didn't got life sentences.

No one lives on the YFZ ranch now, and I am not sure where everyone else went. Maybe back to Short Creek, who knows? Although Warren Jeffs sits in TDCJ, he still has contact by phone with his congregation, and they still follow his commands. With all of the work that we as a team did, nothing really changed except the twelve-year-old child bride was never returned to her parents and remains in the custody of a family who are not members of the FLDS sect.

Over a year of my life was dedicated to this project, and during that time, my eyes were opened to the fact that as much as you want to believe that you are in control of the things you believe, you are not. It seemed there were so many things out in front of us to stop us from protecting these children, but because of it being so high profile, I guess someone with more authority than us made the rules. A year after the raids, the task force had a reunion in San Angelo, and we all had one big feeling in common—anger over going through the things we went through, being placed in danger on the night of April 3, 2008, having to live with the nightmares and dreams of the whole ordeal, and knowing that these children were back with those who were not protective of them.

We were all presented with plaques and little trophies as a token of appreciation for being on the task force. Did we make a difference? I cannot answer that question, but I would like to think that somehow we did. And as for the girl who called the intake in, although I have my doubts about it, the reports were that a young black girl with mental issues in another state called it in. I have questions about that because I am not sure how she was able to describe the things she did regarding the temple, the sect itself, and even more questionable is that FLDS did not associate with black people in any form or fashion and looked at them as being evil. So how did she know the things that she knew?

I can't answer that question. I wish I could. The only thing that I can say for certain is that what started out to be something small ended up to be something larger than anyone had ever imagined, and the state of Texas was not prepared for it. There was no organization in the ordeal as a whole. Those who were left in charge really had no idea of what was really going on; they were getting second- and third-hand information, and the whole thing was just one blown-up piece of work, something that will haunt me for the rest of my life.

Many people have said that they were a part of FLDS. Yes, they may have been there for a day, a week, or maybe one of those who helped move the children to foster homes. Everyone who was there was touched in some way by their involvement with what just one man was able to accomplish with his power that he had gained over these people. It is amazing to me that just one name makes me physically ill and brings back so many nightmares from the past—Warren Jeffs. Would I change it and not be a part of it? The answer to that question is—definitely not.

Cross made of wood from the gates of the Ballenger farm

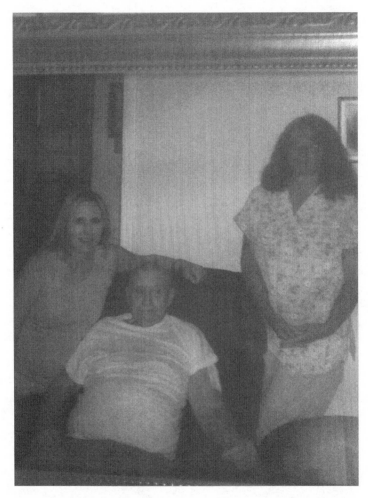

My father on the Father's Day before he passed away

Chapter 15

I wanted a perfect ending. Now I've learned the hard way that some poems don't rhyme and some stories don't have a clear beginning, middle, or ending.

"Life is about not knowing, having to change, taking the moment, and making the best of what it is without knowing what's going to happen next. Delicious ambiguity." —Gilda Radner

As I read this quote, I knew that it would be in the final chapter of my book. It is such a fitting quote because throughout my life, I have found that there is no perfect ending; sometimes you get answers and sometimes you don't. You can't hold on to things forever because the only forever is in eternity—and that comes after you let go of life—and that no matter how many people you know, there are times that you will feel alone.

In my quiet time of the day, I take a moment not to ask God for anything but to thank him for all of the experiences that he has given me, for the things that I have learned from those experiences and the many people who have come and gone from my life who have given me life lessons. In thinking about that, it is then that I know that there is a reason for everything. A reason for certain times in your life, a reason for meeting people, a reason for being at certain places at certain times, and a reason for just being on this earth.

I have never been angry because I lost a husband too early; I have been thankful that I had him in my life for as long as God allowed him to be there. I have never asked God why my first husband cheated on me or why I was a battered woman. I have just taken those lessons as something that made me who I am: a stronger woman. I have lived out my dreams many times over, more than some will ever have the chance to do. I have cried when I am happy, and I have cried when I am sad, but I cry tears because that is what one does when the time is right, and I am not afraid to cry.

My preacher says that God is good all of the time, and he is. There have been times in my life when I was in a place where God wanted me to be, and there were times when I strayed from God. God always brought me back to him, and I am thankful that he is a never-failing God that never leaves his children. I don't question why my daughter chose drugs, but I rejoice in the fact that she is living life again, and she is a special part of life that God gave me.

I believe that God gave me CPS for a reason. From that, I learned that not all life is good. Children are not always safe, loved, and cared for. They sometimes live in a world that no child should ever have to live in. It made me much more aware of what to look for and how to help them if ever the time comes and to communicate that they are precious in his sight always. I am glad that God gave me those final moments to sit with my grandfather, my father, and my husband as they passed from this life into the kingdom of heaven. I saw the peaceful look on their faces as they drew their last breaths, and there is no other place they could be but in the arms of Jesus.

I thank God for that because I know in the end of my life's journey, I will see them again. I know that there is a time and reason for everything. People come into your life for a reason; God's timing is perfect in allowing those people to come into your life when they do. I am thankful for the new life with my husband that God gave me, a life of knowing love and true friendship again. Some questioned me when I remarried, but who are they to question my life? I don't have to answer to them. Our life is good and something that was a part of God's perfect timing. Life may not always be good, but God is good all of the time, and in the end, that is what matters.

Book Insert

It was pitch-dark throughout the compound except for this beautiful white building that was illuminated with lights. It appeared to be a vast building, larger than any building on the premises, appearing to stand taller than any other building. I remember thinking to myself, What a beautiful church. Or at least it appeared to be a church. The roads were winding, and it seemed like we drove for an eternity of twists and turns. I remember thinking to myself, If I have to find my way out of here, head toward the church. I didn't feel that I could find my way out if I had to, even using the "church" as a land marker because it seemed to be in the center of the compound to me. I wasn't sure that I would know where to go from there if I had to find my way out.

We finally arrived at our destination—a place that had been deemed by FLDS members as the place where we could meet with and interview the female children in the sect. It was the school. The building was constructed of logs that appeared to be handmade. As we entered the school building, I was filled with so many feelings: amazed at what I had seen, excited to find out what I could about the abuse, surprised at the things that I was seeing as I went inside the building, and wondering where this would lead. I can remember thinking to myself, This looks larger than a one-hundred-fifty-person compound.

As we climbed up the steps to the cabin-like school building, I noticed that both sides of the steps were lined with men who were modestly dressed in jeans and nicely starched and ironed pastel-colored shirts. Most of them had their hair combed similarly, short and parted to the side, and none of them, although they were polite, had smiles on their faces. And as we entered the building itself, I observed that the hallways were also lined with men on both sides of the wall. I immediately began to decipher that this was an intimidation tactic by them.

Kerrie Bullard